JIM HANCOCK & KARA POWELL

GOOD SEX

STUDENT JOURNAL

WHAT (ALMOST) NOBODY WILL TELL YOU ABOUT SEX

2.0

ZONDERVAN®

ZONDERVAN.com/
AUTHORTRACKER
follow your favorite authors

youth
specialties

youth specialties

Good Sex 2.0: What (Almost) Nobody Will Tell You About Sex
Copyright 2009 by Jim Hancock and Kara Powell

Youth Specialties resources, 300 S. Pierce St., El Cajon, CA 92020 are published by Zondervan, 5300 Patterson Ave. SE, Grand Rapids, MI 49530.

ISBN 978-0-310-28270-9

Cover and interior design by SharpSeven Design

Printed in the United States of America

09 10 11 12 13 14 • 20 19 18 17 16 15 14 13 12 11 10 9 8 7 6 5 4 3 2 1

CONTENTS

INTRODUCTION

Read Me

It doesn't take a genius to know that everything we hear about sex can't be equally true. People say sex is a purely natural and biological urge, so knock yourself out(!). But don't look for any meaning there. Other people say sex is an almost sacramental act of communication between a man and a woman committed for life. And you can find somebody saying just about everything in between...I mean, gimme a break! How's anybody supposed to figure out where the truth lies?

One thing's for sure: Almost no one expects an honest, well-thought-out answer from the church. Your church is probably very cool about sex, but most seem to have lost their voices on the subject. Some churches are speechless because they're just as confused and afraid about sex as everyone else. Other churches scream themselves hoarse defending positions that aren't necessarily all that clear in the Bible. And parents (not yours, of course, but plenty) are about as helpful as most churches. Some are just scared silent; others have talked so much they have laryngitis. In either case we see their lips moving, but it's hard to make out what they're saying. So a lot of us stop listening.

Wouldn't it be nice to have a reasonable, direct, honest, genuine, hopeful conversation about sex? Wouldn't it be great to talk about God's gift of sex in optimistic (but not unrealistic) terms? Wouldn't it be wonderful to mention sex without fear or anger or pretending? Or waiting for the lecture that's sure to follow?

Well, it would be nice, and it's entirely possible. Not easy, maybe, but entirely possible. It's why we wrote this book.

Here are some of the Big Ideas behind *What (almost) Nobody Will Tell You about Sex:*

- We're created in God's image, male and female.
- Sexuality is a wonderful, complex gift that takes a lifetime to explore.
- Sex touches every part of us—our bodies, sure, but also our minds, emotions, spirits, and every relationship from our families to the God who makes us sexual (and everyone in between).
- Sex is affected by our brokenness and wrongdoing, just like everything else about us.
- Sex can be rescued and renewed by the grace of Christ, just like everything else about us.

What (almost) Nobody Will Tell You about Sex is designed to help you understand your sexuality in the broad context of your whole life.

If our strategy is to look at sex in the context of the whole person, then our *tactics* involve a collection of self-contained-but-still-connected elements—bite-sized experiences to get you thinking and writing and talking and deciding what you want to do with God's gift of sex.

What (almost) Nobody Will Tell You about Sex is organized into seven sections, plus The Stuff at the Back of the Book:
- **Sex Messaging**: responding to the cultural messages you're wading through (or maybe more accurately—swimming through)
- **Sexual Identity**: thinking about the forces that shape your sexuality
- **Intimacy**: dating and nonsexual closeness
- **Desire**: understanding your appetites and needs
- **Boundaries**: deciding what to do with your sexuality
- **Responsibility**: taking sexual responsibility
- **Do-Overs**: experiencing mercy, repentance, forgiveness, and restoration
- **The Stuff at the Back of the Book**: Plumbing + Wiring FAQs, Back-to-Basics Biology, How to Help Victims of Sexual Abuse and Other Tough Stuff, and All the Sex in the Bible

Each section includes a short essay and a collection of things to think about, write about, and maybe even talk about.

NOW | The stuff labeled NOW focuses on what people want (or say they want) and the way people tend to behave when left to their own devices.

NEW | The stuff labeled NEW focuses on understanding what the biblical texts say about sexuality and how they can be applied to transform people and relationships.

HOW | The stuff labeled HOW focuses on what we can do as individuals and groups of friends to help each other grow into our sexuality healthy and whole.

There's a logic to the order of *What (almost) Nobody Will Tell You about Sex*, but don't let the table of contents keep you from where you want to go. If you feel the need to jump straight to Do-Overs because you or a friend are in need of a fresh start, then do it (it's not like you need our permission). If you know someone who's the victim of sexual abuse, then don't start on page one—go straight to The Stuff at the Back of the Book.

REAL-WORLD SEXUALITY

In the real world, we encounter sexual information and experiences in a process that stretches over decades. Out of that process—or in the middle of it—we construct our ideas and values about sex.

Most of that information—and quite a bit of the experience—is indirect. We read, listen, watch television and movies, and hang out with siblings, friends, and acquaintances. We watch our parents and other adults. We experience sexual arousal for the first time (and it takes us by surprise!).

Out of all these impressions, we construct a picture of what sex is—or appears to be. And, out of that picture, our sexual attitudes, opinions, and actions emerge. The picture is updated each time we encounter new information and experiences and, even in adulthood, the picture is never complete as long as we're learning.

Just for grins, take a moment to compare that process of learning about sex with most *teaching* about sex. Most of what kids get directly from adults is much less a process than a confrontation: *Here are the facts, remember them. This is the truth, believe it. These are the boundaries, don't cross them.*

If experience is the best teacher (not our favorite teacher, maybe, but the most effective), then which of these will be more influential: *process* or *confrontation*?

What (almost) Nobody Will Tell You about Sex is a process rather than a confrontation because we're convinced that's how people really learn.

Once we reach puberty, we're always talking about relationships with the other gender. We're exposed to films, books, magazines, music, and television shows in which sex plays a big role. We live in a human context that's often, on one level or another, about sex. It's all part of the process—except at church (and a few other adult-sensitive settings) where grown-ups confront instead of process. Come to think of it, that is part of the process, whether or not it's a conscious choice. That's one reason kids grow up believing it's not safe to talk about sex when adults are around.

LET'S JUST GET THIS OUT ON THE TABLE

Our culture, our bodies—every fiber of our beings—scream for sex early and often. Early and often is not exactly a biblical approach to responsible, intimate, self-disciplined, pleasurable, committed, passionate sex. So we're in a bit of a bind: Either our culture and our bodies are right about sexual fulfillment (and God just forgot to mention it), or God is perfectly clear about the sexual experiences that are most fulfilling, useful, helpful, and ultimately pleasurable, and we simply have a tough time understanding how everything works.

An ancient Hebrew ritual celebrates a fascinating process of leading children into loving obedience to their invisible Creator:

> Hear, O Israel: The Lord our God, the Lord is one. Love the Lord your God with all your heart and with all your soul and with all your strength. These commandments that I give you today are to be upon your hearts. Impress them on your children. Talk about them when you sit at home and when you walk along the road, when you lie down and when you get up. Tie them as symbols on your hands and bind them on your foreheads. Write them on the doorframes of your houses and on your gates.
>
> —Deuteronomy 6:4-9

Now *that's* process. Sitting around the house; walking around the block; bedtime stories and morning devotions; a bracelet on your arm; a do-rag on your head; all day, every day, thinking about God and what God wants. People who get wrapped up in what God wants tend to do what God wants; in the same way that people who get wrapped up in what they want tend to do as they please. Funny how that works.

Here's another idea from the Bible: "Do not conform any longer to the pattern of this world, but be transformed by the renewing of your mind. Then you will be able to test and approve what God's will is—his good, pleasing and perfect will" (Romans 12:2, NIV). *What (almost) Nobody Will Tell You about Sex* is a process between you and God and, if you like, a few people you really trust.

To encourage that process, we also created a process for youth groups called *Good Sex: A Whole-Person Approach to Teenage Sexuality and God*. It's a resource that invites whole groups to consider, understand, and surrender their sexuality to the God who loves them and made them sexual.

The youth group process covers everything in *What (almost) Nobody Will Tell You about Sex* (and quite a bit more) in the context of group interaction and support. Your youth group leader can get the *Good Sex* Leader's Guide and DVD online and wherever Youth Specialties and Zondervan books are sold.

This book won't answer every question about sex. How could it? Instead, it's loaded with great questions to help you wrestle with God's truth and your own experience.

And that's the combination that makes the difference: God's truth shaping your experience. Dive in. Enjoy. Let us know what you think.

SEX MESSAGING

Session 1

THE BIG IDEA

> Now suppose you come to a country where you could fill a theatre by simply bringing a covered plate on to the stage and then slowly lifting the cover so as to let every one see, just before the lights went out, that it contained a mutton chop or a bit of bacon, would you not think that in that country something had gone wrong with the appetite for food?[1]

C. S. Lewis wrote that in the 1940s. We think he was on to something. We think maybe something has gone wrong with our appetite for sex. Pretty much any way you look at it, our culture is preoccupied with sex way out of proportion to its actual significance.

You've grown up largely unprotected from what grown-ups cynically refer to as "adult content." But you didn't introduce all of that to the equation, did you? No, that would be your parents' generation—and your grandparents' and possibly even your great-grandparents' generation—who did that.

So what can we do to help you understand and enjoy and take responsibility for your sexuality? How do we equip you for life in the world where you live (not in some Neverland where people don't wrestle with sexuality)?

It's a little embarrassing to admit how poor a job the generations just ahead of you have done at this. We've had too many sexual partners, spread too many sexually transmitted diseases, gone through too many divorces—not all of us, of course; just too many of us.

Sometimes we didn't know what we didn't know. And sometimes we knew and chose poorly. It's no shock that we—and often you—have paid a price for that. Sorry. We could use some generational do-overs, if you're willing to give them.

It doesn't make sense to tell you how much things have changed because, for you, they *haven't*. You've never known a world without HIV/AIDS and other widespread sexually transmitted diseases. You've never lived in an age without easy access to porn. As far as you're concerned, marriages have always had about a 50-50 chance of making it. The world is what it is. If your generation stops the spread of those diseases, if you ignore pornography and it goes away because it's disgusting and demeaning, and if you create strong marriages that last a lifetime, then that won't be considered "going back to a better time." If you do those things, then you'll be going *forward*. Forward is the direction of hope, which is what you should mainly be concerned with every day.

There are people—you already know this—who think it's odd to introduce the Bible into a conversation about sexuality. Why, they wonder, would you bring something written so long ago and far away to what must be a 21st-century discussion? It is, after all, the 21st century…

Our answer is that what the Bible says about sex may actually be more helpful today than ever. Most everybody—including us—agrees that things are messy these days. But not messier than what's recorded in the Bible. The earliest Christian communities flourished in cultures where sexual behavior was flat-out abusive. Those folks lived in places where sexual slavery was a given and where women and girls were property—collected, traded, used, and discarded. They lived in cities where boys were sex objects for wealthy men. And no one raised an eyebrow, let alone a helping hand.

> You never change anything by fighting it; you change things by making them obsolete through superior technology.[2]
> — Buckminster Fuller

People who loved Jesus stood out in those cultures. And it wasn't so much about what they said as the way they lived. God's people reinvented the family by living in committed marriages, instilling respect for women, and protecting and nurturing children instead of exploiting them.

Think about how many abused people become abusers. If it's always been that way, and there's every reason to believe it has, then that means that from the beginning of the Christian faith there were abused people who somehow found the strength to break the cycle of abuse because they loved Jesus. They chose to give better than they got.

That was world-changing stuff—not because smart people wrote about it but because ordinary people lived it out.

Maybe it's time to do that again. People who claim to know something about God have a reputation for telling others what to believe and how to behave—but not necessarily taking their own advice. We've reached the point where almost nobody listens anymore because actions speak so much louder than words.

So maybe it's time to stop talking so much—especially about other people's behavior—and quietly, steadily help each other grow into our own sexuality healthy and whole. We can do that with God's grace—not because we're good but because *God* is so very good.

This Journal begins with Sex Messaging. Because Job One is sorting through all the messages you've received about sex your whole life—the good, bad, and indifferent—so you can pitch the ones that are garbage and embrace the sex messaging that is true and noble and right and pure and lovely and admirable. (That last part is borrowed from Philippians 4:8, which sort of sums up our hope for you in this Journal.)

Okay, then. Here we go…

NOW | Where Did You Learn about Sex?

Q: Do you think it's true that people get the "clean" info about sex from their parents and the "dirty" version from kids at school? How would you even define clean, and how is that different from the "dirty" version?

Q: How comfortable do you think parents are talking to their own kids about sex?

Totally   Sort of   Not Even

Because...

Q: How comfortable do you think kids are talking to their parents about sex?

Totally   Sort of   Not Even

Because...

Q: How would you rate the quality of information you've received about sex from your friends?

Completely Reliable   Not Bad   Completely Unreliable

Because...

Q: How would you rate the quality of information you've received about sex from health-care professionals?

Completely Reliable   Not Bad   Completely Unreliable

Because...

Q: How would you rate the quality of information you've received about sex from TV shows and movies?

Completely Reliable   Not Bad   Completely Unreliable

Because...

Q: How would you rate the quality of information you've received about sex from your parents?

Completely Reliable   Not Bad   Completely Unreliable

Because...

Q: How would you rate the quality of information you've received about sex from magazines and books?

Completely Reliable   Not Bad   Completely Unreliable

Because...

Q: How would you rate the quality of information you've received about sex from siblings and cousins?

Completely Reliable   Not Bad   Completely Unreliable

Because...

Q: How would you rate the quality of information you've received about sex from classes at school?

Completely Reliable   Not Bad   Completely Unreliable

Because...

Q: How would you rate the quality of information you've received about sex online?

Completely Reliable   Not Bad   Completely Unreliable

Because...

Q: Have you been hurt by any bad information?

• If so, what was the source of the bad information?

• What happened?

• How did you feel about that?

• How did you work it out?

• Did you have anyone to help you process that?

Q: Is there any source of sexual information you consider so poor that you simply won't go there? Why is that?

• Is there any source of sexual information that's so consistently helpful you'd recommend it to someone who needs help? If so, what makes it so valuable to you?

Q: So far, where have you found the most reliable and helpful sexual information? Why do you think that is?

Q: Some people would say the sexual messages in the Bible are mainly negative. Why do you think people have that opinion?

Q: On the whole, how would you rate the quality of sexual information you've received from your church or directly from the Bible so far?

☐ First-rate information because…

☐ Pretty good information because…

☐ So-so information because…

☐ Not-so-great information because…

☐ Awful information because…

NEW | Soft Hearts

Read Mark 10:1-12.

Q: What point do you think Jesus was making in his response to these religious leaders?

Q: Do you recognize the biblical passages Jesus quotes here: "God 'made them male and female'" and "'For this reason a man will leave his father and mother and be united to his wife, and the two will become one flesh'"?

The first quotation is from Genesis 1:27—
> So God created human beings in his own image,
> in the image of God he created them;
> male and female he created them.

The second quotation comes from Genesis 2:24—
> For this reason a man will leave his father and mother and be united to his wife,
> and they will become one flesh.

When the religious leaders challenged Jesus with the law of Moses on divorce, Jesus responded by going back to the first principles in creation:
1. Men and women are both created in God's image.
2. The union of a woman and a man in marriage is not a disposable relationship.

Q: Why do you think either idea was ever in question?

William Barclay says the problem Jesus was addressing hinged on this fact:
> In Jewish law a woman was regarded as a thing. She had no legal rights whatever
> but was at the complete disposal of the male head of the family. The result was that
> a man could divorce his wife on almost any grounds, while there were very few
> on which a woman could seek divorce. At best she could only ask her husband to
> divorce her. "A woman may be divorced with or without her will, but a man only
> with his will."[3]

Q: "It was because your hearts were hard that Moses wrote you this law," Jesus said (Mark 10:5). How does a person with a *soft heart* treat someone he loves?

• How long do you think someone can fake that?

• How do you think adolescent romance would change if relationships were governed by genuinely soft hearts for each other?

• How do you think the marriages you're familiar with would improve if they were governed by genuinely soft hearts for each other?

Q: Consider the characteristics you associate with a soft-hearted person:
• How does a soft-hearted person listen?

• What does a soft-hearted person look for in someone she loves?

• What kinds of things does a soft-hearted person do for someone he loves?

Read 1 Corinthians 13 and write about soft-hearted love.

Q: Let your imagination go for a moment: If an extraterrestrial being—an angel, for example—had been watching you for the last six months, what would he or she say about your heart?

Mushy   Soft   Firm   Hard   Stony

• What evidence would that conclusion be based on?

HOW | Can | Be Perfectly Honest with You?

Suppose you wanted help to understand and grow into your own sexuality healthy and whole. List the characteristics of individuals or a group of friends that would help you trust them with your stories, beliefs, fears, regrets, and hopes.

• Rate yourself on each of the characteristics on your list—10, high; 1, low.

• Name the people, peers and adults you think you can trust to talk to about sexuality.

Q: Confidentiality is square one. Who have you seen hurt because someone told stories about them—true or false—to people who had no business knowing?

• If you've been on the hurting or the being-hurt end of that, write about what happened.

All that said, there's one circumstance when confidentiality is not appropriate—when you're convinced that someone's life is in danger.

If you believe someone's life is in danger:
- Ask a parent you trust—yours or your friend's—to help you get assistance.
- Tell a youth leader or pastor—and no one else.
- If you can't track down a youth leader or pastor, tell a school counselor, teacher, or administrator you trust—and no one else.
- If all else fails and you're honestly afraid for someone's life, dial 911 and explain that you believe your friend is an immediate danger to himself or herself or to others.

For more on helping a person in trouble—including some reliable 800 numbers, if you need them—go to pages 159-161 in The Stuff at the Back of the Book section.

NOW | Loveline

Maybe you've listened to *Loveline*. It's a nationally syndicated radio show (still on the air and streaming on the Web at this writing) originating from Southern California. *Loveline* is readily available to anyone with a radio or an Internet connection. Callers check in from across the nation to talk about sexual issues with Dr. Drew Pinsky and his cohost and guests. Questions and answers on *Loveline* are pretty much no holds barred, so if you ever tune in, be forewarned.

We're not recommending *Loveline*. It can be disturbing and glib and crude even when it's honest, compassionate, and helpful. Use your best judgment.

Here's a sampling of callers from a *Loveline* episode.

> #1: Adam, 18 years old, calls in and says that when he was 16, he slept with his high school English teacher about 10 times. She got pregnant not long after and refused to have any more contact with him. He saw the baby recently and says it looks exactly like him. He's sure the baby is his, but he doesn't know what to do.

Q: What advice do you imagine the *Loveline* hosts gave Adam? Why do you think that?

Q: What advice do you imagine your youth leader would give Adam? Why do you think that?

Q: What do you think Jesus would say to Adam? Why do you think that?

> For a summary of the answers these callers received, see the *Loveline* Answer Sheet on page 162.

> #2: Toni, a 25-year-old female transvestite, calls in to ask for some advice. She slept with a girlfriend's fiancé. The girlfriend has no idea that her future marriage partner is thinking about becoming a transvestite as well. Should Toni tell her friend what she knows?

Q: What advice do you imagine the *Loveline* hosts gave Toni? Why do you think that?

Q: What advice do you imagine your youth leader would give Toni? Why do you think that?

Q: What do you imagine Jesus would say to Toni? Why do you think that?

#3: Melissa, 19, says she was at a house with three male friends, when they spiked her drink with a speedball (part heroin, part cocaine). When she'd completely lost control of her senses, these three so-called friends gang-raped her. That was six months ago. Since then, Melissa has had compulsive sex with more than 30 men— all one-night stands. She doesn't know why she's doing this.

Q: What advice do you imagine the *Loveline* hosts gave Melissa? Why do you think that?

Q: What advice do you imagine your youth leader would give Melissa? Why do you think that?

Q: What do you think Jesus would say to Melissa? Why do you think that?

NOW I RU Sexualized?

Read the following and underline important words, phrases, and sentences.

Societal messages that contribute to the sexualization of girls come not only from media and merchandise but also through girls' interpersonal relationships (e.g., with parents, teachers, and peers). Parents may contribute to sexualization in a number of ways. For example, parents may convey the message that maintaining an attractive physical appearance is the most important goal for girls. Some may allow or encourage plastic surgery to help girls meet that goal. Research shows that teachers sometimes encourage girls to play at being sexualized adult women or hold beliefs that girls of color are "hypersexual" and thus unlikely to achieve academic success. Both male and female peers have been found to contribute to the sexualization of girls—girls by policing each other to ensure conformance with standards of thinness and sexiness and boys by sexually objectifying and harassing girls. Finally, at the extreme end, parents, teachers, and peers, as well as others (e.g., other family members, coaches, or strangers) sometimes sexually abuse, assault, prostitute, or traffic girls, a most destructive form of sexualization.

If girls purchase (or ask their parents to purchase) products and clothes designed to make them look physically appealing and sexy, and if they style their identities after the sexy celebrities who populate their cultural landscape, they are, in effect, sexualizing themselves. Girls also sexualize themselves when they think of themselves in objectified terms. Psychological researchers have identified self-objectification as a key process whereby girls learn to think of and treat their own bodies as objects of others' desires. In self-objectification, girls internalize an observer's perspective on their physical selves and learn to treat themselves as objects to be looked at and evaluated for their appearance.

— Report of the American Psychological Association Task Force on the Sexualization of Girls[4]

Q: What are the most significant things you underlined?

• Why do you think those are significant?

• When and where have you seen examples of what this report describes?

Q: In your opinion what are the five worst sexualizing forces in our society?

Q: Are there any positives to sexualization?

• What do you think is the biggest problem with sexualizing people?

SEXUAL IDENTITY

Session 2

THE BIG IDEA

The first pages of the first book of the Bible say God made humans male and female. Women and men are a matched set. Both are necessary for reproduction; each benefits from the uniqueness of the other. That's sex; that's gender. Two X chromosomes deliver a female; an X and a Y produce a male. Different body chemistry, different physical structures—it's not rocket science.

Sexual identity is a different matter. Sexual identity is how we experience our sexuality, and what we think and how we feel about that. And then what we do about it. This has a lot to do with hormones—testosterone in boys and progesterone in girls. But it also has something to do with how we're treated by our families, friends, schools, mass media—the whole culture. That's what this section is mainly about.

Our families and friends and communities influence how we think about our sexuality from the day we're born. Women and men tell boys and girls how to act; we watch adults and learn how it's really done. And we read, listen to the radio, go to the playground, and watch TV shows and movies. Bit by bit we come to understand ourselves as males and females, which determines, for the most part, how we play and dress and talk and relate to other people.

All is well in the neighborhood. Until puberty hits like a flash flood, and we're up to our hips in hormones and high water.

Chubby boys grow angular; their voices crack and drop; muscles mass and occasionally cramp in places where there didn't even used to *be* places; hair sprouts like patches of grass; unanticipated erections ambush them by day, and erotic dreams produce involuntary ejaculations of semen by night. It is, without question, a crazy time of life.

Skinny girls find their straight lines replaced by curving hips and bellies; their breasts bud and grow (evenly, they hope); they experience unexpected attention from much older males; new hair grows on them, too—although generally not as densely as on their brothers; and they cross their fingers, hoping against the odds they'll be safe at home when they menstruate the first time. These are exceedingly strange days for girls morphing into women.

Such explosive change blows sexual perceptions all over the map. Some of us seem utterly unself-conscious about our sexuality; others are conspicuously self-aware.

In the locker room, one boy saunters to the shower wearing nothing but a smile and a towel around his neck. The boy at the next locker wraps a towel around his waist like a kilt and holds on tight because there's a towel snatcher roaming the aisles of metal lockers. On the way they pass a kid who doesn't need a towel because there's no way he's going near the shower.

In the classroom a girl, dressed for comfort, is oblivious to the boy who sits behind her, transfixed by the curve of her bare shoulder. The girl in front of her is dressed to get attention and seems fully aware of her effect on boys: "She ain't got much," another girl whispers to her friend, "but it's all out there where they can get a look at it." At the back of the room, for reasons that are private and painful, another girl wears baggy clothes to hide her sexuality.

And so it goes in adolescence; the unconscious and the hyperconscious, questioning, defining, and redefining their sexual identity.

What do you want to know about your sexual identity? Here's a short list of things that kids everywhere seem to wonder:
- Am I normal?
- Are my sexual responses normal?
- Why do I get nervous around people of the other gender?
- Why do I get turned on so easily?
- Do I get turned on like other people?
- Why do I feel guilty about my sexuality?
- Am I a sex fiend?
- Am I gay?
- Could I turn gay?

This list hasn't changed much in the last 50 years. Curiosity about homosexuality may have escalated a bit—kids generally talk about homosexuality more comfortably than their parents did back in the day. Other than that, the list looks about the same.

Grown-up responses to these questions haven't changed much, either. Adults who sit down for reasonable, biblically informed conversations about sexuality are few and far between.

Some adults are just plain uncomfortable talking about sexuality. So they challenge a question with a question:

> "Whadaya mean, 'Do you get turned on like other people?' You're not supposed to get turned on at all!"

> "Why in the world would you even ask if you could turn into...one of those?"

> "Is your what too small? What kind of question is that?"

> "You had what kind of dream? I don't think that's even in the Bible."

At this point it will be no surprise to you that Christians don't always agree about sexuality. In fact, Christians can be downright *disagreeable* on the subject.

Take gender roles, for instance.

Some Christians think being male means one thing and one thing only. And being female means the exact opposite. There are male jobs (thinking, heavy lifting, bringing home the bacon) and female jobs (cooking the bacon, cleaning, bearing and raising children) because that's the way God likes it. Anybody who crosses the behavioral divide has some explaining to do.

Other Christians think the only differences between men and women are cultural and therefore nonbiblical, if not frankly *un*biblical. They think we make up what it means to act like women and men as we go along, from one culture to another. As far as those folks are concerned, gender is defined by people's plumbing and wiring; but their behavior isn't (men can nurture without being feminine; women can think without being masculine).

People in these two camps have been known to wonder if the people in the other camp are even Christians.

Or take homosexuality:
- Some Christians think homosexuality is a perversion, plain and simple (like sacrificing babies to a pagan god).
- Some think homosexuality is a complex sin (like alcohol dependency).

- Some think homosexuality is a biological abnormality (like a mutant gene).
- Some think homosexuality is a normal genetic trait (like blond hair).
- Some think homosexuality is a lifestyle choice (like voting Republican).

Jam all those opinions into one room, and things get pretty noisy. Or very quiet. For a lot of Christians, it's easier to not have the conversation at all.

That's a mistake. Maybe this goes without saying, but if we don't decide what we think about sexual identity, then someone else will tell us what to think. In fact, someone else already *is*—loud and late into the night. So we'd better decide.

NOW | SexID

Take a few moments to describe your sexual identity in the following SexID rectangle. Use words, pictures, symbols, or whatever else is comfortable for you. If you get stuck, some of the questions below might help you.

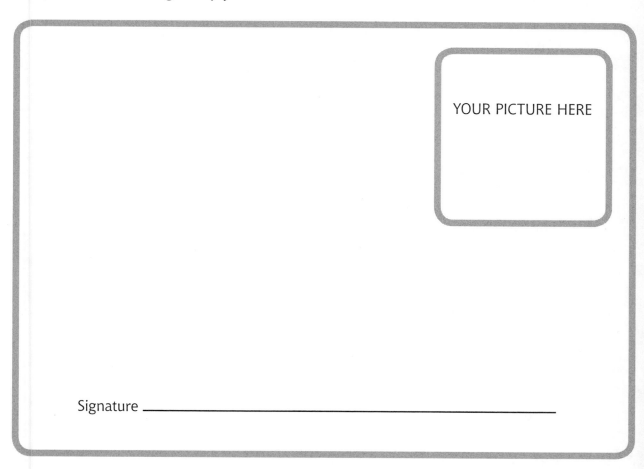

YOUR PICTURE HERE

Signature _____

Q: Do you feel it took you a short time or a long time to describe your sexual identity in the SexID rectangle? What does that tell you about yourself?

Q: What are the most important things you wrote on your SexID?

• What do you feel is missing?

Q: How has your sexual identity been shaped by the following? Write as much as you want; skip any that don't apply.

- Family

- Classmates

- Teachers

- Church or youth group or Christian events

- Coaches

- Employers

- Television or movies

- Books

- Magazines

- Music

- Internet

- Radio

Q: What role do you think God plays in what you wrote on your ID?

- What role would you like God to play?

HOW | New Creation

Here's a simple way to think about the story of our lives with God: Good/Guilt/Grace/Gratitude.

Chapter One: Good—We're all created in God's image, male and female, and it's a beautiful thing.

Chapter Two: Guilt—Motivated by pride, we've all done things we're not proud of—ironic isn't it? More importantly, we've broken faith with our Creator, with each other, and with ourselves.

Chapter Three: Grace—God's attitude and action toward humankind is full of grace and mercy and forgiveness. The way of Jesus leads us back to good faith with our Creator, each other, and ourselves.

Chapter Four: Gratitude—Everything about us (including our sexuality) is an opportunity to express eternal gratitude to the God who made us and refuses to lose us—the One who pursues us and rescues us from our pride and craziness by the work of Jesus.

Q: Can you recall or find biblical passages that contribute to these chapters in God's Story?

• Good:

• Guilt:

• Grace:

• Gratitude:

As you think about this Good/Guilt/Grace/Gratitude story, how does it relate to any sexual issues you're dealing with now? Jot down your thoughts in this new version of your SexID. If you get stuck, some of the next questions might help you.

Good

Guilt

Grace

Gratitude

YOUR PICTURE HERE

Signature _____

Q: Which of these four chapters in God's Story do you understand the best? How is that helping (or hurting) you with your sexual choices?

• Which of these four chapters still puzzles you? How is that affecting your sexual choices?

Q: Has admitting your Guilt and embracing God's Grace made a difference in your sexual identity?

• Why or why not?

• With what sexual struggles and questions do you still need to depend on Jesus for help?

Q: It's been said that pride and laziness are two ways we often break faith with God, ourselves, and others. Can you see any ways in which pride or laziness keeps you from fully embracing God's Story and gaining a healthier sexual identity?

• How do you think embracing Jesus as your Rescuer would affect your view of yourself and your sexual identity?

Q: If you haven't already admitted your Guilt and asked Jesus to rescue you by his Grace, then what questions or unresolved issues are keeping you from doing that now?

Q: Do you agree that when it comes to sexuality, half of the church whispers, and half of the church shouts? Why or why not?

• Which extreme have you experienced more? How has this affected you?

• Besides gender roles and homosexuality, what other sex-related areas do church people disagree on? Why do you think that is?

As mentioned on page 28, here's a (partial) list of questions adolescents have asked about for as long as anyone can remember:

- Am I normal?
- Are my sexual responses normal?
- Why do I get nervous around people of the other gender?
- Why do I get turned on so easily?
- Do I get turned on like other people?
- Why do I feel guilty about my sexuality?
- Am I a sex fiend?
- Am I gay?
- Could I turn gay?

Q: What other questions do teenagers ask about sexuality?

Q: What are some questions about sexuality (maybe they're on the list; maybe they're not) that you've had answered?

Q: Where did you get those answers?

Q: What are the questions about who you are sexually that you still don't have answered?

NOW | Like Father, Like Son

Q: How, if at all, are the sexual-identity messages you're receiving from your family different from those that other families give?

Q: What are the most helpful messages about sexual identity you've received from your family?

• What are the least helpful messages about sexual identity you've received from your family?

Q: What have you learned from your family about sexual identity that you intend to pass on to your children?

• What have you learned from your family about sexual identity that you'd rather not pass on to your children?

Q: Is there anything about your sexual identity that you wish you could talk about with someone? If so, what do you have to gain or lose by having that conversation?

NOW | The "H" Word

Q: Why do you think homosexuality is such a volatile issue in our culture?

Q: Do you think there's any difference between homosexual curiosity and homosexual identity? If so, what's the difference?

• Have you had any homosexual or bisexual curiosity or experiences?

Q: If someone close to you said he thought he might be a homosexual, how would you respond?

Q: If someone close to you said she no longer wanted to identify herself as a homosexual, how would you respond?

Q: What questions do you have about homosexuality or bisexuality?

• With whom would you talk about those questions?

NOW | The Grass Is Browner

It seems when people get indignant about other people's wrongdoing, it's usually about issues they don't share. For example, someone may get more upset about homosexual experimentation (a temptation he's never experienced) than pornography (a temptation he knows quite well).

Q: How much truth do you think there is in that observation?

• Have you ever been on the receiving end of this kind of thing—harshly judged by someone who suffers from a different set of temptations?

• Have you ever been on the judging end—being hard on someone whose temptation you didn't understand, while going easier on someone with whom you identified more closely?

Q: You've probably heard the phrase "Love the sinner and hate the sin." Here's a twist on that phrase: "Love the sinner and hate your own sin." What's good about that twist? What's bad about it?

Q: Do you wrestle with a temptation that leaves you feeling isolated?

• If you have that kind of struggle, and if you were going to let someone in on it, do you know someone who might be a safe person? (Meaning someone you believe will really hear you, give you good counsel, and keep your sharing confidential.)

Q: If you know someone struggling with a temptation that isolates her, what could you do to become a safe and helpful confidant for that individual?

• Take a moment to pray for that person right now.

NEW | Fruit: A Manly Meal or a Feminine Treat?

Q: Do you ever wonder if you're as masculine (or as feminine) as you're supposed to be?

Q: Who are the best models of masculinity you know?

• What makes their masculinity appealing?

Q: Who are the best models of femininity you know?

• What makes their femininity appealing?

Read Galatians 5:22-23.

Q: Do you generally think of anything on that list as seeming more masculine than feminine or vice versa?

• If so, which strike you as more masculine and which seem more feminine?

	More feminine because…	More masculine because…	Both feminine and masculine because…
Love			
Joy			

Peace			
Patience			
Kindness			
Goodness			
Faithfulness			
Gentleness			
Self-control			

Q: Think back on the past year. Which of the Spirit's fruit would you say are more abundant in your life today than a year ago? How do you feel about that?

Q: Do you think any of the Spirit's fruit are less abundant in your life today than a year ago? How do you feel about that?

Please read the following thoughts about Jesus, femininity, and masculinity:

Jesus combined what we call masculine and feminine traits in a comfortable balance of humanness. He hugged children and spoke up for them in Mark 10:13-16. He got physical with merchants who exploited poor people in the temple in John 2:13-22. He was tough on people who were full of themselves in John 5:41-47. He cried over the grief of a friend in John 11:35. Jesus was not a stereotypical, testosterone-crazed man, and he wasn't a sissy. In a culture where children were disposable and women would have been second-class citizens, had they been allowed to be citizens at all, Jesus respected children and treated women as equals. And the spirit of Jesus, the Holy Spirit, produces fruit in every believer's life as if gender had nothing to do with anything.

The fruit of the Spirit is love, joy, peace, patience, kindness, goodness, faithfulness, gentleness, and self-control. When it comes to our sexual identity, God's Spirit nullifies "boys will be boys" and "women—can't live with 'em, can't live without 'em." The Holy Spirit replaces roughness with gentleness and transforms compulsiveness into self-control. Not quickly, perhaps, but inevitably.

This is not to say there's no difference between men and women, only that the differences have nothing to do with character, giftedness, or fruitfulness. Does this make sense in our culture where people are stereotyped from the moment of birth? Not really. But so what? As Jesus put it to Nicodemus in John 3:8, "The wind blows wherever it pleases. You hear its sound, but you cannot tell where it comes from or where it is going. So it is with everyone born of the Spirit." The people of God—male and female—are freaks; we don't fit cultural norms because we're coming from another place. Our passports are issued in the kingdom of heaven where we're—every one of us by God's grace—naturalized citizens.

That means that in our culture, women may be considered masculine and men may be thought feminine for exhibiting characteristics that are merely godly. And it breaks our hearts (on those days when it doesn't make us angry) that these characterizations are about as common inside the family of God as outside. We can't control what outsiders say about us, but shame on us for choosing cultural stereotypes over biblical models of transformation and growth. That's just plain wrong.[5]

Q: How does that passage confirm what you were thinking?

• How does that passage challenge what you were thinking?

Q: In what ways does our society force gender norms upon us?

Read Galatians 3:26-29.

Q: How much sense does it make to suggest that Paul was saying we lose those things that make us men and women when we become followers of Jesus Christ?

• What do you think he's actually getting at?

Q: What do you think we have to gain or lose by treating each other first as humans made in God's image, and then as male and female? Write about that.

• What do you think we have to gain or lose when we either accept or take a pass on the gender norms of our culture? Write about that.

NOW | That's Gotta Hurt

Q: To what degree would you say the following have influenced your sexual identity?

	Zero Degree	To Some Degree	A Great Degree
Physical disability			
Verbal and emotional abuse			
Violent physical abuse			
Sexual molestation			
Rape			
Incest			
You name it:			

Q: If you've been the victim of any of these wrongs, who knows about it besides you and the person(s) responsible?
☐ Nobody else knows.
• If this is true, then do you think it might be better to let someone in on this? What do you have to gain or lose?

☐ I have great support from people who can really do something to help.
• If this is true, then how did they find out about your need?

- What do those people do that is helpful?

- What have you learned from them about helping people in pain?

☐ Other people know, but they couldn't (or wouldn't) do anything to help.
- If this is true, then how did they find out about your need?

- Why do you think they couldn't or wouldn't help?

- Describe how you feel about not getting the help you need.

Q: Do you know someone whose sexual identity has been influenced by any of the following factors? Check all that apply.
☐ Physical disability
☐ Verbal and emotional abuse
☐ Violent physical abuse
☐ Sexual molestation
☐ Rape
☐ Incest
☐ You name it: _____

Q: Do you believe you can do anything to help this person?

Q: As you finish this reflection, is there anything you need to do in response to what you've been thinking about?

- If so, then what do you think you have to gain or lose by taking that next step?

INTIMACY

THE BIG IDEA

Sex does not equal intimacy. Intimacy equals intimacy. What's so hard about that?

Well maybe it's hard because most of us don't really know what intimacy means, let alone how to be intimate.

Intimacy grows between people who trust each other with their deepest natures. Intimacy rejects fakery and shortcuts. There's no such thing as instant intimacy—instant attraction, yes; instant crushes, of course; but real intimacy takes time. You can tell you're in an intimate relationship if you both choose being real instead of faking it; being warm instead of being cool; understanding instead of judging—not every day, maybe, but most of the time, for a long time.

The feelings that come with intimacy can be huge, spanning the distance from inexpressibly glad to unspeakably sad, from the hollow ache of separation to the giddy joy of reunion.

But intimacy isn't a feeling; it's a condition. Intimacy takes time and attention and energy. To some people, that sounds a lot like work. So, sometimes people do things to *feel* intimate, even if they aren't. It's rumored that some girls are interested in sex because it makes them feel intimate. (It's also rumored that some boys fake intimacy in order to get sex.)

It doesn't take a genius to understand what happens when people pretend to be intimate: Intimacy Lite—less filling, but still intoxicating in sufficient quantities.

It also doesn't take a genius to understand why people might settle for Intimacy Lite. True intimacy is risky. Being intimate means facing the possibility of rejection and embarrassment. If I reveal the truth about me, then I risk the possibility that you'll say, *Ewwww! That's creepy.* Which, needless to say, is painful. And if you tell other people that I'm creepy, then the pain rises to the level of humiliation—who needs that?

That's why intimacy is so hard: because it's a high-risk investment. And every successful investor knows that Rule One is, "Don't risk more than you can afford to lose."

So after we get hurt a couple of times, most of us learn to lie back and play it safe, investing a little bit of our true selves, but not enough to risk a serious loss.

> Fool me once, shame on you; fool me twice, shame on me.

It's a good strategy, except for the fact that humans need intimacy—whether we want it or not.

Right from the start (Genesis 2:18), God declared that humans shouldn't be alone; we need help to make it. God said, plain as day, that it's not good for humans to be isolated. Most of us know instinctively that God is right about this. Dangerous as it is, what people crave—perhaps more than anything else—is authentic intimacy.

But it turns out that sex can be a handy substitute for authentic intimacy.

There's no question that sex feels intimate. You're breathing the same air, sharing the same space, being glued together sexually—"glued together" is how the Bible puts it when it says two people are united as "one flesh." (See Genesis 2:24; Matthew 19:5-6; Mark 10:7-8; 1 Corinthians 6:16; and Ephesians 5:31. Translated as *cleave* in the King James Version and *united* in the TNIV, the word means, "to glue together.") It's hard to get any closer than that.

But when a relationship comes unglued, so do the feelings. And sometimes the people come apart as well. Here's how a tenth-grade friend expressed her loss:

> my heart is locked
> the key is gone
> one took the key first
> but he mocked my inner strengths
> and beauties
> then he threw away my key
> and left me open to all
> many came
> all went

48   **What (almost) Nobody Will Tell You about Sex**

finally I took the key
and locked me back up
not allowing anyone to enter
and threw away the key
one kind person ventured
under the trash that had piled
high over my key
he was considerate enough
to find my key
which no one had time to find
he started to open me
but didn't get very far
then he left
like every one else in
this human world of
imperfection
I will not allow anyone
in my heart
for a long time

Do you ever wonder why dating—the way most of us do it—doesn't work very well? Why the shortest distance between a blissful crush and wishing you'd never met someone is going out with that person?

Going out can be a messy business. (This is just a general observation; skip this part if you think you're the exception to the rule.) Here's how most dating breaks down:

Phase One: Guess Who?

The mess begins when someone—let's call her Sophie—tries to figure out what sort of person the sort of person she wants to go out with wants to go out with. Are you following this?

Generally, Sophie has someone in mind—Joaquin or Billy Joe or Shaquille or Haing (could be anyone)—chosen because he's cute or looks like he needs rescuing or whatever.

Phase Two: Masquerade

Sophie figures out what Mr. Stud Muffin wants and says, I can be that. Then she fakes her way to romance. Sooner or later, directly or indirectly, Sophie tells a lie to maintain the masquerade. It's doomed from the start; anyone can see that. The only thing missing is the voice of that lady from the old TV sitcom laugh tracks saying, "Uh-oh!"

Phase Three: Getting Serious

Getting serious is easy to spot: Just look for two high school juniors acting like married people (except they live with their own parents). Neither can make plans without consulting the other; they cross the borders of married sexual behavior; they can't talk about where they'd like to be in five years without getting their feelings hurt; they buy stuff together. Sophie finds it's easier to "make love" (which makes her feel close, temporarily at least) than talk seriously with her Stud Muffin, which is frustrating in the extreme.

Phase Four: The Cinderella Syndrome

Eventually, the clock strikes 12, and Sophie turns into a pumpkin. It's humiliating and sad, and she feels she's lost something she can't replace. She's distracted (or intensely focused), she can't sleep (or can't wake up), she gains some weight (or loses weight rapidly). For a while, Sophie wonders if she'll make it. But after a few weeks, she thinks it's probably just as well because she never really enjoyed pretending to be a Cowpunk-Choirgirl-Skate-Rat anyway. The Muffin was a jerk; how could she not have seen that? Sophie makes a mental note not to get so emotionally involved next time. If there is a next time.

One day, out of the blue, Sophie wonders—again—what sort of person the sort of person she wants to go out with wants to go out with. You following this?

No wonder some people try to drain the emotion from sexuality.

But it doesn't work. This is the message of countless soap operas, sitcoms, movies, and books (including the Bible). No matter what people say about casual sex, in the end it's quite personal. If you don't believe it, keep watching.

Now here's a funny thing: For people who want to take the intimacy out of sex, we're awfully busy sexualizing intimacy these days. Many in our culture believe intimacy leads inevitably to sex. "You can't get that close to people without going farther," they say. And by going farther, they mean getting sexual. This is intimacy as foreplay, and it's highly toxic to otherwise healthy friendships. (Have you noticed how when people get sexually involved with their close friends, they tend to drift apart afterward?) There goes the possibility of friendship between men and women.

Too bad. The Bible describes us (Christians, at least) as brothers and sisters. Sorry, but there are things healthy brothers and sisters don't do, and it's not because they're not intimate. They've shared a bathroom, for goodness sake. They've had the measles together. They've fought like cats and dogs and then made up because, underneath it all, they love each other. They've lain awake giggling on Christmas Eve, too wired to sleep. They've nursed each other through tough times with Mom or Dad. That's fertile ground for intimacy, and it's the relational model for Christians in community. Sex messes that up something terrible.

Even same-gender intimacy is threatened by the assumption or fear that people can't get close without getting busy with each other. Not everybody makes that assumption—not by a long shot. It's crazy and unfair. But it's there like a rumor, isolating people, making them uncomfortable and suspicious and separate. Again: too bad.

It's not supposed to be like this because it's not good for people to be isolated. God said so.

NEW | Friends with Benefits

Consider the following statements:

Statement 1: I've seen someone wronged or taken advantage of in a relationship.
☐ I totally disagree because…

☐ I'm not sure because…

☐ I agree completely because…

Statement 2: I've been personally wronged or taken advantage of in a relationship.
☐ I totally disagree because…

☐ I'm not sure because…

☐ I agree completely because…

Statement 3: I've seen someone wronged or taken advantage of by a Christian brother or sister while in a relationship with that person.
☐ I totally disagree because…

☐ I'm not sure because…

☐ I agree completely because…

Statement 4: I've been wronged or taken advantage of by a Christian brother or sister while in a relationship with that person.
☐ I totally disagree because…

☐ I'm not sure because…

☐ I agree completely because…

Statement 5: I wish I could take something back that happened in a relationship.
☐ I totally disagree because…

☐ I'm not sure because…

☐ I agree completely because…

Statement 6: I've seen a Christian brother or sister wrong or take advantage of someone in a relationship who isn't (or wasn't) a follower of Jesus.
☐ I totally disagree because…

☐ I'm not sure because…

☐ I agree completely because…

Statement 7: My most intimate friends share nearly all of my most deeply held beliefs and values.
☐ I totally disagree because…

☐ I'm not sure because…

☐ I agree completely because…

Statement 8: The idea of going out with someone whose beliefs are very different makes me nervous because, sooner or later, I know we'll clash over something important and one of us will have to compromise to hold on to the relationship.
☐ I totally disagree because…

☐ I'm not sure because…

☐ I agree completely because…

Ancient Greek talks about four different kinds of love—two of which appear prominently in the New Testament.

- *Agape* (a-gah-pay) is the unconditional love God shows us, and the unconditional love we can likewise show to others (see 1 John 4:7).

- *Philia* (fill-ee-ah) is affectionate love for a friend (see Romans 12:10), from which we get the name *Philadelphia* (a.k.a. The City of Brotherly Love).

- *Eros* (air-oss) is sexual love, from which we get the word *erotic*. (The word *eros* doesn't appear in the New Testament, but the idea is all over the Jewish Scriptures—especially the Song of Songs.)

- *Storge* (stor-gay) is the love shared in healthy families. (This word is also absent in the New Testament but present in spirit.)

Here's what C. S. Lewis has to say about the four loves:

> [Love] is called Agape in the New Testament to distinguish it from Eros (sexual love), Storge (family affection), and Philia (friendship). So there are four kinds of love, all good in their proper place, but Agape is the best because it is the kind God has for us and is good in all circumstances. There are people I mustn't feel Eros towards, and people I can't feel Storge or Philia for: but I can practise Agape to God, Angels, Man and Beast, to the good and the bad, the old and the young, the far and the near. You see Agape is all giving, not getting.[6]

Q: If someone asked you how to keep a healthy balance between the four loves in a dating relationship, what would you say?

• How about in a friendship?

Q: Think back a year and compare where you were then with where you are now in regard to each of the four loves:
• Family love
☐ Worse then because…

☐ About the same because…

☐ Better then because…

• Friendly love
☐ Worse then because…

☐ About the same because…

☐ Better then because…

• Erotic love
☐ Worse then because…

☐ About the same because…

☐ Better then because…

- Agape love

☐ Worse then because…

☐ About the same because…

☐ Better then because…

Q: Given what you've just written, which of the four loves needs the most work in your life?

- Are there things you'd like help to do differently?

NEW | One Another

Circle or underline what we're supposed to do for each other.

• "'Do not steal. Do not lie. Do not deceive one another.'" (Leviticus 19:11)

Q: What happens in relationships when people don't steal, lie, or deceive?

• "'Administer true justice; show mercy and compassion to one another.'" (Zechariah 7:9)

Q: What is the life expectancy of relationships marked by justice, mercy, and compassion?

• "Salt is good, but if it loses its saltiness, how can you make it salty again? Have salt in yourselves, and be at peace with each other." (Mark 9:50)

Q: What do relationships sound like when people are at peace with each other?

• "A new command I give you: Love one another. As I have loved you, so you must love one another." (John 13:34)

Q: What kind of relational problems do people face when they love each other as Jesus loves them?

• "Be devoted to one another in brotherly love. Honor one another above yourselves." (Romans 12:10, NIV)

Q: Do you think people ever get tired of being honored by others who are devoted to them in brotherly love? (That's the *philia* we talked about a few minutes ago.)

• "Live in harmony with one another. Do not be proud, but be willing to associate with people of low position. Do not be conceited." (Romans 12:16, NIV)

Q: Can you name two (or several) people who live in harmony with each other? Describe what their relationship is like.

• "Accept one another, then, just as Christ accepted you, in order to bring praise to God." (Romans 15:7)

Q: Is there someone who accepts you as Christ does? What's that like?

• "I myself am convinced, my brothers and sisters, that you yourselves are full of goodness, filled with knowledge and competent to instruct one another." (Romans 15:14)

Q: What happens to people in relationships where each one uses his or her strengths to help the other one learn and grow?

• "You, my brothers and sisters, were called to be free. But do not use your freedom to indulge the sinful nature; rather, serve one another humbly in love." (Galatians 5:13)

Q: Is there any downside to serving each other in love, rather than each person indulging in selfishness at the expense of others?

• "Be completely humble and gentle; be patient, bearing with one another in love." (Ephesians 4:2)

Q: How messed up does a person have to be to abuse someone who's completely humble, gentle, and patient?

• "Be kind and compassionate to one another, forgiving each other, just as in Christ God forgave you." (Ephesians 4:32)

Q: What happens to God's reputation when people follow Jesus in expressing kindness, compassion, and forgiveness to each other?

• "Therefore encourage one another and build each other up, just as in fact you are doing." (1 Thessalonians 5:11)

Q: Do you have a friend who lends you courage when you need it? And to whom you return the favor when that person's running a courage deficit? What's that like?

• "Make sure that nobody pays back wrong for wrong, but always try to be kind to each other and to everyone else." (1 Thessalonians 5:15, NIV)

Q: How do you think your group can see to it that nobody pays back wrong for wrong?

• "And let us consider how we may spur one another on toward love and good deeds." (Hebrews 10:24)

Q: What happens when someone puts the spurs to you, stimulating you to love and serve?

• "Therefore confess your sins to each other and pray for each other so that you may be healed." (James 5:16)

Q: Do you know what it's like to have friends listen to your humble confessions as acts of mercy and healing? Write about that…

• "Above all, love each other deeply, because love covers over a multitude of sins. Offer hospitality to one another without grumbling. Each of you should use whatever gift you have received to serve others, as faithful stewards of God's grace in its various forms." (1 Peter 4:8-10)

Q: How attractive is a spiritual community where deep love covers over a multitude of sins, where hospitality is genuine, and where each person uses God's gifts to serve the others?

Repellent   Moderately Appealing   Incredibly Attractive

• Make a list of people you know who'd find that type of spiritual community attractive.

NOW | Intimacy

Q: What's your definition of *intimacy?*

• How did you come up with that definition?

Q: How is intimacy different from lust?

Q: Do you think intimacy is more of a "woman thing" than a "guy thing"? Why?

Q: Do you think intimacy almost always leads toward sex?
☐ Absolutely not because…

☐ Maybe, maybe not because…

☐ Absolutely because…

Q: Do you think sex is the most intimate act that humans can perform?
☐ Absolutely not because…

☐ Maybe, maybe not because…

☐ Absolutely because…

Q: Have you made mistakes with intimacy? Write about that.

• If so, what did you find out about yourself?

• What did you find out about someone else?

• What did you find out about intimacy?

Q: When you think about intimacy, which attitudes and emotions apply?
☐ Anticipation because…

☐ Fear because…

☐ Regret because…

☐ Hope because…

Q: What differences (if any) do you see between intimacy with someone of the same gender and intimacy with someone of the opposite gender?

Q: What do you still have to learn about intimacy?

• From whom do you think you might get help?

• How could you ask for that help?

What (almost) Nobody Will Tell You about Sex

NOW | Love Stories

Q: Describe the relationship of the most maturely intimate couple you know.

• When you observe that relationship, how do you feel about your own future?

• What do you think you'd have to do to get what they have?

Q: If this couple isn't your parents, how do you imagine their love stories compare to your parents' relationship?

• If you marry, how do you imagine your relationship with your spouse will be different from your parents' relationship? Why?

Q: What would you say your past and current relationships contribute to your preparation for future intimacy?
☐ Very little because…

☐ Not as much as I wish because…

☐ Quite a bit because…

☐ I don't know what more I could ask for because…

Q: Are there any fresh commitments you need to make to prepare yourself for intimacy in the future?

NOW | Mistakes Girls Make

The following is a list of mistakes some girls make when they relate to guys.[7] How often do you see these mistakes?

   A—All the time
   S—Sometimes
   N—Almost never

When a girl is lonely or insecure…

A   **S**   **N**   She often doesn't really choose; she just goes out with whomever is available.

A   **S**   **N**   She throws herself at guys to get attention.

A   **S**   **N**   She works at making herself unattractive to lessen the pain.

When a girl likes a guy…

A   **S**   **N**   She nags the guy's friends to see if he might like her back.

A   **S**   **N**   She flirts; if he doesn't notice, she flirts even harder.

A   **S**   **N**   She plays it cool and aloof, hoping the guy will notice how cool she is.

When a girl starts dating a guy…

A   **S**   **N**   She's too busy making sure he wants her to question whether or not she wants him.

A   **S**   **N**   She expects him to be a knight in shining armor who will rescue her from all bad things and protect her from all harm.

A   **S**   **N**   She plays it cool and aloof, hoping the guy will notice how cool she is.

A   **S**   **N**   She thinks he'll stop behavior that bugs her.

A   **S**   **N**   She thinks she can change him.

A   **S**   **N**   She lets him be her life instead of a part of her life.

A   **S**   **N**   Her fear of abandonment makes her clingy.

A   **S**   **N**   She trades physical gratification to get relational gratification.

A   **S**   **N**   She cuts herself off from her family.

A   **S**   **N**   She cuts herself off from her friends.

When a girl goes through a breakup…

A   **S**   **N**   Instead of taking some time apart to recover, she still tries to spend time with him as friends and keeps opening old wounds and repeating old mistakes.

Q: Why do you think girls make these mistakes?

Q: Which of these mistakes are the most costly in terms of sadness, self-doubt, and loss of self-esteem?

Q: What can you and your circle of friends do to help girls recover from these mistakes?

• What can you and your friends do to help girls avoid these mistakes?

NOW | Mistakes Guys Make

The following is a list of mistakes some guys make when they relate to girls.[8] How often do you see these mistakes?

A—All the time
S—Sometimes
N—Almost never

When a guy is lonely or insecure…

A   **S**   **N**   He gets obnoxious around girls because he tries too hard.

A   **S**   **N**   He acts pitiful, hoping a girl will feel sorry for him.

When a guy likes a girl…

A   **S**   **N**   He lets her looks blind him from seeing who she really is.

A   **S**   **N**   He shows off, usually in macho ways, trying to impress her.

A   **S**   **N**   He is hyper-attentive, acting like she's the only person on earth.

When a guy starts dating a girl…

A   **S**   **N**   He tries to be a knight in shining armor who will rescue the helpless damsel from all bad things and protect her from all harm.

A   **S**   **N**   His girlfriend becomes a badge of honor instead of a real person.

A   **S**   **N**   He seeks physical gratification before relational gratification.

A   **S**   **N**   He lets her take care of him, more like a mother than a girlfriend.

A   **S**   **N**   He tries to control her and make decisions for her.

A   **S**   **N**   He confuses being macho with courage.

A   **S**   **N**   He continues in the relationship without ever evaluating its quality.

A   S   N   He tells her what he thinks she needs to hear to have sex with him.

A   S   N   He cuts himself off from his family.

A   S   N   He cuts himself off from his friends.

When a guy goes through a breakup…

A   S   N   He doesn't get advice from people who could help.

A   S   N   He walks out too quickly.

A   S   N   He tries to hold on too long.

A   S   N   He gets depressed or angry and takes it out on himself or others.

Q: Why do you think guys make these mistakes?

Q: Which of these are the most costly in terms of sadness, self-doubt, and loss of self-esteem?

Q: What can you and your circle of friends do to help guys recover from these mistakes?

• What can you and your friends do to help guys avoid these mistakes?

NEW | One Is the Loneliest Number

Q: If you're going out with someone now (or have in the past), what do you think your closest friends would say about that relationship?

• Have you asked your friends' opinions about this person's effect on you? Why is that?

Q: How do you think your closest friends would say this person is affecting (or has affected) your relationship with God?

• Have you asked for your friends' opinions about that person's influence on your relationship with God? Why is that?

Q: (Assuming this applies) If you were your own best friend, what would you say about your spiritual influence on the people you've gone out with?

• What would you say about your spiritual influence on the person you're going out with?

Q: Have you had any experience, positive or negative, with group dating—several individuals doing things together without pairing up?

• What do you think group dating might contribute, positively or negatively, to intimate relationships?

Q: Think about your closest friendships for a moment. How do those relationships affect your intimacy with God?

• How do you think you affect your friends' intimacy with God?

Q: Can you think of one thing you could do in a dating relationship or friendship that would help you both grow closer to God?

• What would you have to gain by that?

• Would you have anything to lose?

NEW | Best Buds

Q: What makes your closest friends your closest friends?

Q: Think for a moment about what's happened in your friendships in the last year. When has intimacy been easier?

☐ When good things happen to my friends, because...

☐ When good things happen to me, because...

☐ When bad things happen to my friends, because...

☐ When bad things happen to me, because...

☐ When we've spent more time together, because...

☐ When we've spent less time together, because...

☐ Circumstances don't seem to matter, because...

In the passage you're about to read, Jonathan is the son of the king of Israel and first in line to succeed his father. Jonathan is also the best friend of David who's been unofficially named as the next king, even though he has no legal right to the title.

Read 1 Samuel 20.

Q: Whom do you identify with most in this story? Why is that?

• Whom would you least like to trade places with? Because...

Q: Have you had a friend like Jonathan?

• Have you *been* a friend like Jonathan?

Compare 1 Samuel 20 with 1 Corinthians 13:4-7.

Q: How do you think Jonathan and David stack up in the comparison?

• Compare your closest friendships with 1 Corinthians 13:4-7. How do you think you stack up?

• Do you see anything you could use some help with? Is there someone you know who may be able to help you?

NEW | The Yoke's on You

Read 2 Corinthians 6:14 to 7:1.

Some people cite this passage as a reason why Christians shouldn't go out with people who aren't Christians. In fact, some folks say Christians shouldn't partner in business—or even cultivate deep friendships—with people who don't pledge their allegiance to Christ.

The imagery of being yoked unequally recalls the commandment in Deuteronomy 22:10 to not plow with an ox and a donkey yoked together—there are some animals that just don't fit together because their body shapes are completely different.

Q: Do you think there's a difference between close friendship and being yoked with another person? Write about that.

Q: Do you think this passage means we shouldn't be friends with people who aren't Christians? How would you use what you know about other passages of Scripture to help explain your answer?

• Do you think an unequal yoke could make it difficult for you to lead another person to faith in Christ? Because…

Q: What reasons have you heard to explain why someone who loves Jesus shouldn't go out with someone who doesn't?

• What reasons have you heard to explain why it's okay for Christians to go out with people who are skeptical about the Christian faith?

Q: Do you think you've ever been unequally yoked with another person? If so, write a brief outline of the beginning, middle, and end of that story (if it's over).

• Beginning
Being unequally yoked started when…

• Middle
I realized I was unequally yoked when…

• End
Things unraveled when…

Q: Have you ever been influenced by a friend in a way that you regretted later? Write about that.

Q: Have you ever been influenced by a friend in a way that you still appreciate—even though that person is no longer in your life? Write about that.

Q: If someone asked you to describe the friends who've made a positive difference in your life, what would you say about them?

• How does your description compare to—
—people you've gone out with in the past?

—the person you're going out with now?

—the kind of person you'd like to go out with?

—the kind of person you want to become?

Q: Have you ever influenced a friend in a way that he appreciated (and you later found out about it)? Write about that.

• Have you ever influenced a friend in a way that she came to regret? Write about that.

Q: Can you think of an area where you'd like to grow to become a better friend?

HOW | Will You Go Out with Me?

It's hard for some people to ask someone out. It's hard for others to gracefully decline an invitation.

Q: If you're a girl, do you feel comfortable asking a guy out?

Q: If you're a guy, how would you feel if a girl asked you out?

• How easy is it for you to do the asking?

Q: What scares you about asking someone out?

• Do you have a horror story about asking someone out?

• How about a horror story about being asked out?

Q: Have you ever accepted a date because you didn't know how to decline the invitation?

• If so, why was it hard to decline?

• How did things turn out?

• Did you learn anything useful from the experience?

Q: What's the best way to ask someone out?

Q: If you've ever been turned down, what did that feel like?

Q: What's the best way to decline a date?

HOW | Breaking Up (Is So Very Hard to Do)

If you haven't been through a breakup, make your observations about the worst breakup you've seen up close.

Q: What's your worst breakup story?

Q: What do you think it takes for a breakup to go well?

• What do you think is the biggest barrier to that happening?

Q: If you've gone through a breakup, on a scale of 1 (not so bad) to 10 (way worse), how painful was it compared to the greatest emotional pain you've ever felt?

Q: Did you go a little nuts after your breakup? Mark any of these that apply:
☐ I gained weight.

☐ I drank heavily.

☐ I rebounded into an unhealthy relationship.

☐ I felt suicidal.

☐ I lost weight.

☐ I started biting my nails.

☐ I got into fights.

☐ I had trouble sleeping.

☐ I slept too much.

☐ I felt sexually compulsive.

☐ I had trouble concentrating.

☐ I had trouble with my grades.

☐ I had angry blowups.

☐ I isolated myself from others.

☐ I hated being alone, so I constantly surrounded myself with people.

Q: What did it take for you to come out on the other side?

• How long did that take?

• Who contributed to your recovery?

• Where do you think God was in all that? How did that make you feel?

HOW I Kiss Dating Goodbye?

Q: On a scale of 1 (really bad) to 10 (couldn't be better), how would you rate your experience with dating so far?

• What do you think would make going out a better experience for you?

Q: If someone asked you to explain why you date the way you do (or why you don't date), how would you respond?

Q: If you're going out but you're not happy with your dating patterns, what do you think would make that better?

Q: Suppose you kissed traditional dating goodbye. What problems might that create for you?

• Suppose you choose to follow a stereotypical dating pattern. What problems might that create for you?

• Would going out in the conventional sense solve any problems for you?

Q: There's an assumption that we're either dating, or we're spending a lot of lonely nights. Write about that assumption as it relates to true intimacy.

Q: How compatible is American-style dating with building true intimacy?
☐ Completely compatible because...

☐ Needs work, but compatible because...

☐ Completely incompatible because...

DESIRE

Session 4

THE BIG IDEA

Desire is good. Except when it's bad.

Think about it. Desire drives one person to sacrifice herself in pursuit of a cure for AIDS. Desire drives another person to indulge in behavior that spreads HIV.

Desire is tricky that way.

Healthy desire generates commitment and propels accomplishment. Unhealthy desire, on the other hand (and there's always another hand, isn't there?), fuels lust. And lust, as the book of James says, "gives birth to sin; and sin, when it is full-grown, gives birth to death" (James 1:15). Yikes!

Learning to cultivate healthy desires (and avoid being seduced by unhealthy desires) is what this section is about. It's no secret that it's not as easy as it sounds.

Desire is so easily twisted:
"I like it," becomes "I want it."
"I want it," becomes "I need it."
"I need it," becomes "You owe it to me."
Which becomes "Never mind, I'll just take it."

People get out of control when they get upside down with desire. And maybe that's what unhealthy desire is really about: Seizing control when we don't get what we want, exactly when we want it.

> I've never really been mad at God; God just has the job I want. —jh

Stupid? You bet. Unusually stupid? Not really. Everyone falls under the spell of unhealthy desire at some point.

• A tenth grader with an appetite for fine dining finds himself craving far too much of a good thing because his mood elevates when he eats and falls when he's hungry.

• A senior, who likes a tidy room, becomes so obsessed with neatness that no one comes over anymore—which is fine with her since people are such slobs anyway.

• A ninth grader, who started out enjoying physical pleasure as much as the next person, takes a wrong turn into sexual compulsion and doesn't even know how it happened, let alone how to get back to the main road.

Food, tidiness, pleasure—it's all good. But when desire turns bottom side up, beautiful things turn ugly.

It's not hard to see what unhealthy desire does to relationships. Let's face it, most of us are young and inexperienced, no matter how mature or sophisticated we appear to be. Look for the telltale signs in others:

• They get selfish and pushy when the one thing they desire is the very thing (or experience, or relationship) they can't have. Watch for aggressive or obnoxious behavior (not hostile, necessarily, but disagreeable nonetheless).

• Those who believe they're entitled to more than they get start taking more than they give. Watch for foot-dragging, lateness, incomplete follow-through, testing limits, whining, and other passive resistance. Listen for reports from their friends of loyalty tests, tongue-lashings, and ultimatums.

• When folks feel something is being withheld from them, they get sneaky and secretive. Look for lying, cover-ups, and burning bridges.

• And look for someone on the other side of the relationship who says (sooner than later, we hope), "Who needs that? I'm outta here."

This is a critical moment. The young man or woman with the courage to withdraw from someone whose desire is out of control needs support and encouragement. That person's commitment to health will almost certainly be tested.

The one struggling with unhealthy desire also needs care. Because the next stop may be isolation, followed by obsession, maybe even perversion.

Don't leave anyone high and dry if you can help it. Look for signs of withdrawal, isolation, substance abuse, violence, and other high-risk behavior. Use your network of friends to draw that person out. Give him an invitation to vent feelings without giving false hopes of rekindling the flame (remember, he was playing with fire to begin with). If you detect signs of obsession—telephone hang-ups, stalking, self-mutilation—consider bringing in a trustworthy adult (not someone who'll freak, someone who'll help).

> The world breaks everyone and afterward many are strong at the broken places.[9]
> — Ernest Hemingway, *A Farewell to Arms*

Unhealthy desire leaves its mark. A lot of us remain vulnerable, many for the rest of our lives. It may be more or less intense, but it's nearly always baffling. Some people are surprised to learn how many of us expect to struggle with unhealthy desire until we die. That's probably because Christians haven't been talking about that kind of thing lately. But they used to.

The apostle Paul told his flock in Corinth that God used some kind of persistent problem (he didn't give details) to keep him from getting conceited. Paul says he pleaded with God to take it away again and again, but God said, "My grace is sufficient for you, for my power is made perfect in weakness" (2 Corinthians 12:9). So, Paul said, he came to delight in weakness. He's in a fairly small club—because of his delight, not his weakness.

Some Bible teachers say Paul was referring to some kind of physical weakness, like progressive blindness, and maybe that's right. But lay this passage next to Paul's lament in Romans 7 and see what you get:

> I know that nothing good lives in me, that is, in my sinful nature. For I have the desire to do what is good, but I cannot carry it out. For what I do is not the good I want to do; no, the evil I do not want to do—this I keep on doing. Now if I do what I do not want to do, it is no longer I who do it, but it is sin living in me that does it. So I find this law at work: When I want to do good, evil is right there with me. For in my inner being I delight in God's law; but I see another law at work in the members of my body, waging war against the law of my mind and making me a prisoner of the law of sin at work within my members. What a wretched man I am! Who will rescue me from this body of death? Thanks be to God—through Jesus

Christ our Lord! So then, I myself in my mind am a slave to God's law, but in the sinful nature a slave to the law of sin.

— Romans 7:18-25, NIV

Again, some teachers explain this away; they say Paul is talking about life before he was a Christian. But the evidence suggests another possibility. It's possible that Paul struggled with an unhealthy desire so powerful that only God's grace could overcome it. If that's true, then Paul wasn't alone in his struggle with desire, and the rest of us shouldn't be surprised when we struggle. Because desire is tricky that way.

NOW | Guess Who Is Sexually Active

Q: When do you remember first having sexual thoughts and desires?

• How did you feel about that?

Q: What do you usually think of when you think of a sexually active teenager?

• Do you fit this category?

> I hate it when adults use the term "sexually active." What does it even mean? Am I gonna like deactivate someday, or is it a permanent state of being?
> —Juno MacGuff, in Juno (Fox Searchlight Pictures, 2007)

Q: Are there other ways that you're sexually active?

• How do you typically respond to your sexual desires?

• How do you feel about your typical response?

Q: Are there any ways in which you feel sexually out of control?

Never   Sometimes   Often

• If so—whether it's sometimes or often—write a letter to God about it. If not, then write a letter to God about that.

HOW I SexTalk: Desire

Q: For the average teenager (whatever that means), when is desire good?

• When is it bad?

Q: Which of your own desires do you consider good?

• Which do you think are inherently bad?

• Why do you think they're bad?

Read Romans 7:18-25 (it's on pp. 80-81).

Q: What about Paul's experience is relevant to your own feelings about sexual desire?

Q: In the middle of the sexual desires and tensions you're facing, what would it look like to rely on the "God, who delivers me through Jesus Christ our Lord"?

NOW | Behind the Scenes

Q: Think about your last sexual experience—however you define that. What do you think fueled that sexual experience?

Q: Sometimes insecurity is behind adolescent sexual experiences. How might that be true, or untrue, for you?

• Often fears generate our insecurities. How might your fears contribute to insecurities—which might, in turn, fuel sexual desires?

Q: What do you think God might say to you about your fears, insecurities, and desires?

• What makes you think God would say that?

Q: What, if anything, would you like to do differently when you recognize the fears, insecurities, and anxieties that fuel your sexual desires?

Q: Is there someone you can confide in about this? Why do you think that?

NEW | Is Masturbation Okay?

What does the Bible say about masturbation? Well, nothing directly. The word *masturbation* never appears in the Bible.

Some Christians think masturbation is always wrong because (1) it often involves fantasizing about someone sexually, and (2) it's a form of sexual stimulation, which they believe should be saved for marriage.

Some Christians think masturbation is perfectly all right and a normal way to release sexual pressures.

Some Christians fall somewhere in the middle, saying masturbation may be okay, but it can easily become addictive and controlling, so do it only rarely.

Q: Based on what you know today, would you recommend that someone your age engage in masturbation?

• Jot down a few reasons for your answer.

According to Dr. Mark Laaser, there are three common "building blocks" that lead to sexual addictions: sexual fantasizing, masturbation, and use of pornography. They work together and reinforce each other; pornography stimulates fantasy and masturbation is a way to act out and express a fantasy.[10] Isolation often follows, producing ideal conditions for fantasizing and acting out...and the cycle continues.

Q: How does that Cycle of Addiction relate to your own sexual temptations?

Although the Bible never uses the word *masturbation*, it gives us all sorts of principles that help us know what we should do. Let's start with 1 Corinthians 10:13—

No temptation has overtaken you except what is common to us all. And God is faithful; he will not let you be tempted beyond what you can bear. But when you are tempted, he will also provide a way out so that you can endure it.

Q: How do you think 1 Corinthians 10:13 relates to obsessive or compulsive masturbation?

Gerald May adds this insight to the question of addictive behavior in his discussion of attraction addictions.[11]

Attraction addictions are marked by:
- Tolerance—I need more and more to get the same results over time.
- Withdrawal symptoms—I feel bad if I don't get what I long for.
- Self-deception—I lie to myself with excuses, denials, and other mind games.
- Loss of willpower—I don't know how to control my longing.
- Distortion of attention—My longing interrupts my love for God, others, and me.

Read James 1:13-15.

Q: Do you think compulsive masturbation could fall into the pattern James outlines here? Why do you think that?

- Do you think it's possible to masturbate occasionally, without being dragged into the cycle of addiction? Why do you think that?

Q: If you're in the cycle of addiction right now, whom can you talk to about your struggle?

- When might you be able to talk?

• What help do you hope to receive from that person?

Q: If you know someone struggling with an addiction (sexual or otherwise), how might you be able to help him or her?

WHAT WE'RE NOT SAYING: We're not saying masturbation is always an addictive behavior.

WHAT WE ARE SAYING: Be alert for the signs that Gerald May writes about in *Addiction and Grace:*
• Tolerance: needing more and more to get the same results
• Withdrawal symptoms: feeling bad if you don't get what you want
• Self-deception: lying to yourself with excuses, denials, and other mind games
• Loss of willpower: inability to control your longing
• Distortion of attention: the interruption of your love for God, others, and yourself

HOW | Until I Get Married

Picture yourself on the night before you get married, looking back on your life between now and then. Write a letter from your future self to your current self about how you responded to your sexual desires during the years from now to then. (You following this?) What would your future self be glad you did? What would your future self wish you'd done differently?

Q: Are you concerned about how your current sexual behavior might complicate your life in the future?
☐ Not at all because…

☐ A little because…

☐ Quite a bit because…

Q: How, if at all, do you depend on God's grace to play a part in the way you respond to your sexual desires?

• What do you wish God would do to help you? What makes you hope—or doubt—God will do that?

Q: What's your biggest prayer for your sexual life?

• If you wish to marry, what's your biggest prayer for your future spouse?

BOUNDARIES

Session 5

THE BIG IDEA

The Bible doesn't even acknowledge the one question that people ask most often about sex—at least not directly.

The question goes something like this: "I know I'm not supposed to have sex, okay? But how far can I go? I mean, is it okay to get into scoring position?"

Well…if sex were a game, that would be an interesting question. The point of games is—at the risk of being obvious—to score. It would be a bad thing to finish the inning with runners on base.

If sex were a game.

But sex is less like a game than a super-intimate conversation. Sex is less like a game than a secret whispered between lovers. Sex is almost sacramental. It's like baptism: The visible sign of an invisible reality.

"Fine. I just wanna fool around a little. How far can I go without getting baptized?"

It's a fair question. The trouble is, God doesn't get very detailed about the answer. There's no mention in the Bible of fooling around, nothing about making out. And why is that? Because Bible folk weren't interested in sex? Not likely. Because people got married really young? Umm…maybe. The Bible first spoke into very different cultures than ours, that's for sure.

"FINE! Look, I'm just trying to get a little without having God all mad at me! So, for crying out loud, will you please just tell me, HOW FAR CAN I GO?"

Well, okay. But you may not like the answer because the Bible doesn't really talk about all this in any modern sense. What the Bible *does* talk about—quite a bit, actually—is lust.

So here it is: You may go as far as you wish; as long as you stop before you lust.

???

Lust is a serious fixation on something that's not ours to have; it's a deep, focused, inappropriate craving. In the Bible the images associated with lust are heavy breathing, smoldering, and bursting into flames. The Bible doesn't talk about hooking up; it talks about longing for experiences that aren't rightly ours and breaking boundaries to get them.

This section is about learning to identify and respect sexual boundaries.

The trick is, not everybody lusts the same. Some people can hardly go to an art gallery or ballet without drooling, so forget about watching R-rated films and television. Some people are turned on by the smallest bit of exposed midriff, so that trip to the beach is going to be a problem. Some people can barely endure a hug, let alone a back rub, so youth group cuddling is out of the question. It's just too much to handle (so to speak). For those who lust easily, just being around other people can be a trial; just turning on a computer is a temptation; just going to the pool (or beach or lake) is an ordeal.

Other folks have a much higher lust threshold. (Who knows why?) They take in stride images and touch that drive other people crazy. This is why Christians are called to a high level of sexual sensitivity. It's our duty to look out for each other and do our best to avoid tempting someone who may lust for different reasons than we do.

Now don't go getting all defensive. This doesn't mean girls have to wear clothes that cover from chin to shin. And it doesn't mean boys can't show appropriate affection. It *does* mean we oughta talk to each other about these things.

Most of us are embarrassed about what makes us lust. We have friends who apparently don't lust at all; they watch videos and read books and dress in ways that drive us over the edge. That's a shameful experience.

So why not give each other a break? Why not ask each other about what triggers lust? This is a dangerous question in one way because it may mean giving up a video from time to time; retiring a favorite outfit because the clerk at Abercrombie wasn't kidding when she said it was hot; hugging hip to hip instead of belly to belly. And who really wants to give up anything, even for a friend?

But that's the key, isn't it? Friends sacrifice for each other, just because they're friends. And we're not talking about anything that violates your ability to be *you*. An inconvenience here and there—nothing more.

What if your circle of friends decided to ask each other, "What makes you lust?" It would be time to speak up, wouldn't it? If sexual content in films and television is a problem for you, then that would be your opportunity to say so. If short skirts or bare bellies or low-cut tops drive you to distraction, then that would be an ideal time to admit it. If brotherly hugs ignite unsisterly fires in you, then you could sound off. And it would be okay because you'd find out you're not alone. We have different thresholds for lust, but sooner or later we all lust. Anyone who denies that simply hasn't gotten there yet; or they've decided to lie about it. It's just a matter of time…

Whether or not you and your friends have the courage to talk about lust, you can—and must—create boundaries that protect you from lust. If you can't handle seeing people in bathing suits, stay away from places where folks sunbathe. If some movies and television throw you, politely decline to watch. If the Internet pushes your hot button, move your computer to the kitchen—or at least don't use it behind closed doors. Whatever it takes, okay?

NOW | When Is It Sex?

Q: If someone asked people at your school, "When is it sex?" what do you think the majority would say?

Q: Does the question, "How far is too far?" make sense to the people you know who don't claim any relationship with Jesus? Because...

Q: Say you had a friend who was going out with someone who had different sexual boundaries than she did, and your friend asked for your advice on how to maintain her boundaries. What would you say?

Q: Check the box that you think accurately completes the sentence, "It's not sex until [x] because..."

☐ looking because...

☐ hugging because...

☐ massaging because...

☐ hand-holding because...

☐ kissing because...

☐ caressing because...

☐ mutual masturbation because...

☐ oral sex because...

☐ anal intercourse because...

☐ vaginal intercourse because...

- How did you reach that conclusion?

Q: Whose right or responsibility is it to draw sexual boundaries? Why?

Q: Have you had a disagreement about that with anyone you were involved with? If so…

- What happened?

- How did you feel?

- How did you work it out?

- How do you feel toward that person now?

Q: Do you think there's a way to discover a person's view of sex without having a fight about it?

- How could a conversation about "When is it sex?" be helpful to two people who are going out? Can you think of any harmful effects?

- Do you think you can go out with someone who has a different view of sexual boundaries without somebody getting hurt? Why?

HOW | What Difference Does It Make?

It's interesting how many people make significant decisions about sexual behavior because they don't think (or have forgotten how much) those choices matter.

Respond to these scenarios with your best, most solid, biblical advice.

Scenario 1: Look; I'm not exactly pure as the driven snow. I've done everything else. At this point virginity is just a technicality. I mean really...what difference does it make?

Scenario 2: I'm kind of new to this whole discussion. I already did it with the people I went out with before I was a Christian. It's not like I can take that back...even if I wanted to. Anyway, I'm willing to listen to reason. So tell me what you think: What difference does it make?

Scenario 3: Not that it's anybody's business, but we've been doing it almost as long as we've been dating. The horse is out of the barn; it's too late to turn back. At this point, what difference does it make?

Scenario 4: My mother does it with her boyfriend. And I know she expects me to do it, too, because she left a package of condoms on my bed so...I guess that's what she thinks of me. So what difference does it make?

Scenario 5: We pretty much figure we're married in the eyes of God. You know, *one flesh* and all that. Yes, we're still in school. And yes, we live with our parents. But we prayed together before we did it the first time, so... It's in God's hands—what difference does it make?

Scenario 6: Honestly? I'm afraid Jesus will come back before I have sex, and I don't want to miss out. Besides, I know God will forgive me—I mean he has to; he's *God,* right? So I mean, really, what difference does it make?

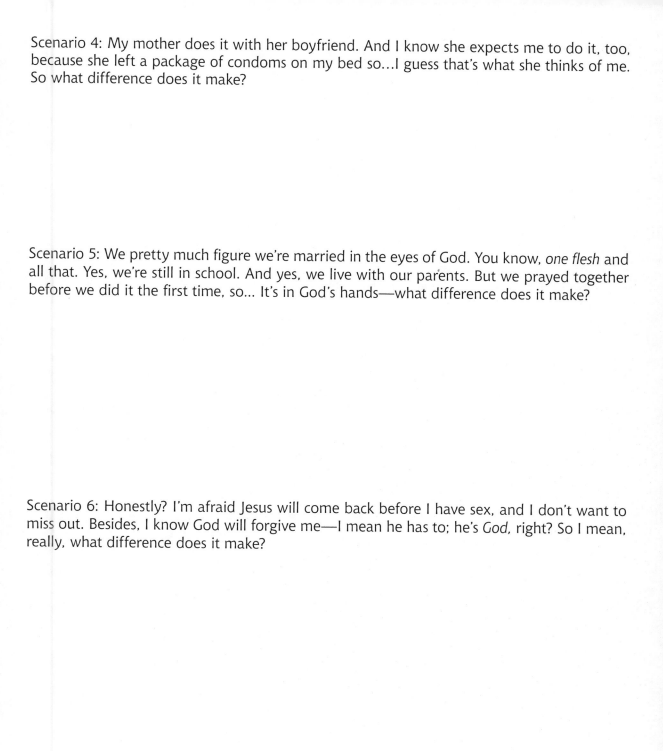

NOW | Dirty Pictures

Here's the origin of the word *pornography:*

ORIGIN mid-19th century: from Greek *pornographos* "writing about prostitutes," from porne 'prostitute' + *graphein* "write."

Q: What has pornography come to mean in your culture?

A Kinsey Institute survey found the top five reasons people say they use porn:[12]
- Number Five: To distract myself (38%)
- Number Four: Because I can fantasize about things I wouldn't necessarily want in real life (43%)
- Number Three: Curiosity (54%)
- Number Two: To sexually arouse myself and/or others (69%)

All leading to...
- The Number One Reason People Use Porn: To masturbate or for physical release (72%)

Q: Are you in any way surprised by those survey results? Or are they about what you'd expect?

Here's another finding from the Kinsey survey.

Among those who use porn...[13]
- 80% say they are fine with their porn use.
- 30% say they feel bad while using porn.
- 19% say they're fine with it, but their partner doesn't (or wouldn't) like them using porn.
- 16% say they feel bad after using porn.
- 9% say they have tried to stop using porn but can't.

Q: What's your reaction to those numbers?

Q: Can you think of anything you and your circle of friends could do to help the 9% of porn users who've tried to quit but can't?

• How about helping the 16% who feel bad after using porn or the 30% who feel bad while using porn?

• How about the people who love the 19% who believe their loved ones don't like them using porn (or wouldn't like it if they knew)?

Q: If you found out that your boyfriend or girlfriend was using porn, how would you feel? What would you say?

• If you found out that a friend was using porn, how would you feel? What would you say?

• If you found out that an adult you respect was using porn, how would you feel? What would you say? What would that do to your level of respect for this person?

Q: Going back up to the first set of findings, if a friend told you she was curious about pornography (like the 54% who say "curiosity" is their motivation for using pornography), what would you say to her, and why?

NOW | What Is Sexy?

Q: Do you think it's okay to be intentionally sexy if you have no intention of having sex? Write about that.

Q: What are the potential benefits and risks of recognizing what's sexy?

Q: Is there anything you find sexy that you'd have difficulty sharing with your circle of friends?

• Why do you think that's difficult to talk about?

Q: Can you recall the first time you found that thing appealing?

• What was going on in your life at the time?

• Can you recall what it is (or was) about that thing that appealed to you?

Q: What's your current feeling about that thing that you find sexy but can't easily talk about?

• Do you ever feel isolated because you find that thing sexy?

• If so, try to think of one person you can trust with this secret.

NOW | Hooking Up, Oral Sex, Friends with Benefits

Q: What do you think "hooking up" is all about? What do you think drives that?

• How about "friends with benefits"? What do you think drives that?

• How big a part do you think oral sex plays in hooking up and friends with benefits?

Here's the final paragraph from an article about girls who kiss each other at parties to get the attention of boys with whom they then hook up.

> "A lot of girls who do want long-term boyfriends will still settle for the hookup because it gives them that temporary feeling of being taken care of and being close to someone," Julie says. "It's sad to see that this is what it's come to—that guys will raise the bar and girls will scramble to meet it. Women just want to know what they have to do to get these guys to fall in love with them. And if guys will take them home after kissing a girl, then that's what they're going to do, because it's better than going home alone." She pauses. "Now that I'm saying it out loud, I'm like, Huh—that's a sad way of going about it."
>
> —Julie, 20-year-old college student[14]

Q: What are your thoughts about Julie's analysis of what lies behind hooking up?

• When Julie says, "It's sad to see that this is what it's come to—that guys will raise the bar and girls will scramble to meet it. Women just want to know what they have to do to get these guys to fall in love with them," do you think that motivation is widespread? If so, do you agree that it's sad? Write about that.

In a 2005 report about casual relationships that involve sex—explicitly described as relationships in which "the two people are NOT serious about each other and are not in love"—here are the top reasons that 13-to-16-year-olds gave for engaging in casual sexual relationships:[15]

- 67% wanted to satisfy a sexual desire.
- 48% wanted to avoid the complications of a serious relationship.
- 37% didn't want to get emotionally involved.
- 37% were curious about this type of relationship.
- 34% wanted to make the relationship closer.
- 33% felt they were too young for a serious relationship.

Q: Reading those responses, what would you say hooking up and friends with benefits was all about?

The same study asked respondents why they had oral sex the first time:

	MAJOR REASON	MINOR REASON	NOT A REASON
• The other person wanted you to do it.	41%	35%	23%
• You met the right person.	47%	24%	29%
• You wanted to satisfy a sexual desire.	36%	34%	30%
• You don't have to worry about pregnancy.	40%	28%	32%
• You were curious.	35%	29%	36%
• You're still a virgin if you have oral sex.	24%	25%	50%
• You wanted to avoid having sexual intercourse.	20%	20%	60%
• You don't think you can get STDs from oral sex.	17%	18%	65%
• You wanted to avoid being touched or undressed.	7%	17%	75%
• You wanted to be more popular and accepted.	4%	17%	79%

Q: Based on those responses, do you see any patterns in the reasons people gave for having oral sex?

Q: Where would you place hooking up on the scale between lust and love?

Lust _____ Love

• Where would you place friends with benefits on the scale between lust and love?

Lust _____ Love

• Given your understanding of the biblical commands about love and lust, what conclusions can you draw about hooking up and friends with benefits?

NEW | Being Careful

A few months after prom, Jimmy told me about deciding to have sex for the first time...

> I guess there wasn't really a moment when I decided, but it was like a process of decisions leading up to it. I'd been going out with this girl for a few weeks. Our physical relationship got way ahead of everything else—we hardly even talked sometimes. I figured sex might just happen if the night was good enough—and prom night is usually kind of special.
>
> I knew I needed to be "careful" so I bought my first condoms. So that's a big step for me, I guess. And when it finally came down to it, it was kind of clinical, actually—there were so many more factors that went through my head. I needed to find a place and a time. A place where we could get alone and no one would find out. It ended up being some kind of an operation, where I had to take care of a whole bunch of logistical factors instead of just letting that moment I'd planned on take control.
>
> I was really at odds with what I was believing and what I was doing. They were two totally different things.

Jimmy's fling at prom was the end of the relationship. A week later they weren't speaking.—*jh*

Q: What stands out for you in this story?

Q: What do you think Jimmy meant when he said what he was believing and what he was doing didn't match up?

Q: What do you think of the argument that says, "If you can't be good, at least be careful"?

• What do you think people mean when they talk about being "careful"?

• What do you suppose God thinks about that?

If you think about the word *careful*, it basically means being "full of care." It's too bad that when it comes to sex, being "careful" has been reduced to making sure you use some form of protection. Protection from what? In reality, being "careful" should mean being full of care for the people involved in your sexual decisions—meaning you, the other person...oh, and God.

Q: Was Jimmy full of care? Did he love the girl he "made love" to?

Q: If he asked if you thought he could make up for his behavior, what would you tell Jimmy?

And then there's alcohol...

> I've had way too many friends who used alcohol as an excuse to go farther than they always said they would.
>
> "I had too much to drink," they say. "I'm not sure how it happened."
>
> I've even heard people say, "I'm not sure what happened. I hope I didn't do anything bad."
>
> A few of them were taken where nobody wants to go because they were drunk.
>
> One girl I know was raped by several boys while she was under the influence at a party. She woke up the next morning sore and hung over. When she realized what went on the night before, she freaked out and spent several days in a psychiatric hospital. It was hard for her to come back from that.
>
> Another friend was raped when she lost at Quarters—a drinking game involving coins and shot glasses, where the loser of each round drinks the shot. My friend and another girl present that day were both attacked. The other girl was sober enough to fight off the boy who climbed on top of her, but my friend was too far gone to

defend herself. The two were so ashamed and afraid of getting in trouble with their parents that they never told anybody. Well, that's not quite true. My friend told me in the hospital after narrowly surviving a very serious suicide attempt. She tried to kill herself after several years of bulimia and sexual craziness. It was another half decade before she started to live a normal life. She's good today, but it was a long slog through a very dark place.

Sometimes I wonder what it is that makes people prefer to not know—or not *seem* to know—what they're doing sexually. And what is it about alcohol that can put people in a position where they can't defend themselves?—*jh*

Q: Does this story sound familiar? How so?

Q: What do you think is going on with people who use alcohol in a way that sets them up or sets others up sexually?

• Have you ever seen that work out well for anyone?

Q: What percent of adolescent sexual encounters do you think just happen with no forethought, no planning, and no setup by either party?
☐ 0% because…

☐ 50% because…

☐ Almost 100% because…

Read Romans 13:9-14.

Q: What strikes you as the most important thing in this passage? Because…

Q: What's the worst thing that comes from thinking about how to gratify the desires of the sinful nature?

☐ Failure to think ahead because...

☐ Unwillingness to think ahead because...

☐ Dishonesty about thinking ahead because...

☐ A little of each because...

☐ Something else because...

Q: How do you think this passage applies to the "I was drunk" excuse?

NEW | Saints Are Made, Not Born

Augustine was an important figure in Christian faith and theology in the fourth and fifth centuries. In his autobiography, *Confessions*, Augustine admits a lengthy (and double-minded) struggle with lust:

> But I wretched, most wretched, in the very commencement of my early youth, had begged chastity of Thee, and said, "Give me chastity and continency, only not yet." For I feared lest Thou shouldest hear me soon, and soon cure me of the disease of concupiscence, which I wished to have satisfied, rather than extinguished.[16]

Continency and *concupiscence* are words from a different era—so let's see if we can clear that up. *Continency* is the ongoing practice of self-restraint, and *concupiscence* means lust. Here's a seat-of-the-pants rephrasing of the paragraph.

> But I, totally clueless at the beginning of adolescence, begged you for chastity, saying, "Give me chastity and self-restraint—only not yet." For I feared you would hear me soon, and soon cure me of the disease of lust, which I wished to have satisfied, rather than extinguished.

Q: So what do think Augustine is getting at?

Commenting on Romans 13:11-14, here's what William Barclay wrote about Augustine's breakthrough:

> The last verses of this passage must be forever famous, for it was through them Augustine found conversion. He tells the story in his Confessions. He was walking in the garden. His heart was in distress, because of his failure to live the good life. He kept exclaiming miserably, "How long? How long? Tomorrow and tomorrow— why not now? Why not this hour an end to my depravity?" Suddenly he heard a voice saying, "Take and read; take and read." It sounded like a child's voice; and he racked his mind to try to remember any child's game in which these words occurred, but could think of none. He hurried back to the seat where his friend Alypius was sitting, for he had left there a volume of Paul's writings. "I snatched it up and read silently the first passage my eyes fell upon: 'Let us not walk in revelry or drunkenness, in immorality and in shamelessness, in contention and in strife. But put on the Lord Jesus Christ, as a man puts on a garment, and stop living a life in which your first thought is to gratify the desires of Christless human nature.' I neither wished nor needed to read further. With the end of that sentence, as

though the light of assurance had poured into my heart, all the shades of doubt were scattered. I put my finger in the page and closed the book: I turned to Alypius with a calm countenance and told him." (C. H. Dodd's translation)[17]

Augustine read from Romans 13:13-14, "But put on the Lord Jesus Christ, as a man puts on a garment, and stop living a life in which your first thought is to gratify the desires of Christless human nature."

Q: First, the second part: What do you think it takes to stop living a life in which your first thought is to gratify the desires of Christless human nature?

• Who do you know who seems to be having some success with that? What can you learn from those people (or that person)?

Q: Now the first part: How do you suppose a person puts on the Lord Jesus Christ as a man puts on a garment?

Q: What do you think you and your circle of friends can do to love each other and look out for each other instead of thinking about how to gratify your own self-absorbed desires?

HOW | Why Wait?

Create two lists.

List One: Reasons ordinary students in ordinary public schools give for having sex when they believe they're ready.

• Are there any reasons you're surprised you've never heard? If so, add them to the list.

• Scratch out reasons that are completely unconvincing to you. Why are they unconvincing?

• Put question marks (?) next to reasons that are sort of convincing. What is it that makes those arguments somewhat convincing?

• Put exclamation marks (!) next to reasons you find very persuasive. What's compelling about those reasons?

List Two: Reasons ordinary students in ordinary public schools give for delaying sex until marriage.

• Are there any reasons you're surprised you haven't heard? If so, add them to the list.

• Scratch out reasons that are completely unconvincing to you. Why are they unconvincing?

What (almost) Nobody Will Tell You about Sex

• Put question marks (?) next to reasons that are sort of convincing. What's somewhat convincing about those arguments?

• Put exclamation marks (!) next to reasons you find very persuasive. What's compelling about those reasons?

Q: How sure are you about what you will and won't do before you're married?

100%   75%   50%   25%   0%

• Why are you at that level of certainty or uncertainty?

• How does that answer compare to where you were at this time last year?
☐ More sure because…

☐ About the same because…

☐ Less sure because…

Q: Have your current convictions been tested?

• How did you resolve that challenge?

Q: What do you think it would take, if anything, to change your convictions?

Ecclesiastes 4:12 reads—
      Though one may be overpowered,
      two can defend themselves.
      A cord of three strands is not quickly broken.

Q: How do you think that idea applies to living true to our convictions about sexual behavior?

• Who else knows the strength of your convictions about this?

• How can you ask that person (or those people) to help you be true to what you believe is right?

HOW | 10 Ways to Say No

Q: How many ways can you think of to turn down someone who wants to take you farther than you want to go sexually? Make a list.

Q: Do you think it's equally difficult for every person to hit the brakes sexually? Why or why not?

• Do you think there are some situations that make hitting the brakes more difficult? Why do you think that's so?

Q: Do you think there's a progression of sexual contact that's assumed by most people when they're going out? In other words, is there a set order in the way a relationship is assumed to develop sexually? If so, what does that look like?

• How soon in a relationship do you think most people would expect to have each of those sexual experiences?

• What makes you think your perceptions about this are reality-based?

• Where do you think these sexual expectations come from?

• Do you think one gender drives these expectations more than the other? Why?

- How do you feel about that?

Q: How do you feel about sexual expectations in your relationships?

Q: If anyone has ever put you in an unfair spot, how did it begin?

• What happened next?

• And then?

• What was going on inside you?

• Is it resolved? Why?

• What's your relationship with that person today?

• How do you feel about those events now?

Q: If you ever put someone in an unfair spot, how did it begin?

• How did it unfold?

• What was going on inside you?

• Is it resolved? Why?

• What's your relationship with that person today?

• How do you feel about those events now?

Q: If you've ever put someone in an unfair spot, do you think you're more or less likely to do it again?

☐ More likely because…

☐ Less likely because…

• Is there someone you can (perhaps even *should*) talk with about this?

Q: If you were to view others as brothers or sisters in Christ, would that affect how you treat them sexually? Write about that.

HOW I SexTalk: Boundaries

Lust is a serious fixation on something that's not mine to have; it's a deep, focused, inappropriate craving. In the biblical languages, the images associated with lust are heavy breathing, smoldering, and bursting into flames. The Bible doesn't talk about hooking up or friends with benefits; it talks about breaking boundaries to get what isn't mine to take.

Q: What kind of damage have you seen lust do to people and relationships?

• Have you been damaged by lust in one way or another?

Q: What are the circumstances in which you're typically tempted to lust for something that's not rightfully yours?

Q: How would you rate your resistance to lust?
☐ Strong because…

☐ Moderate because…

☐ Weak because…

• How do you tend to react when you're tempted sexually?
☐ I tend to deny that I'm being tempted.

☐ I tend to justify myself and come up with reasons why it's okay for me to lust just a little.

☐ I tend to successfully resist sexual temptation.

☐ I tend to call on God for help to resist sexual temptation.

☐ I tend to resist sexual temptation for as long as I can but often give in.

☐ I tend to feel bad about myself for even being tempted sexually.

Q: What could you and your friends do to help each other with your temptations to lust?

Read 2 Timothy 2:22.

Q: How do you understand your responsibility to avoid what tempts you?

Compare that with James 4:7-10.

Q: What does this suggest about your responsibility?

Write a prayer about the temptations you believe you need to flee—at least for the time being.

Write a prayer about the temptations you believe you need to resist—at least for now.

Write a prayer of hope that God will meet you where you are—and take you step by step to where you need to be.

HOW | Does Faith Matter?

The National Survey of Youth and Religion found that sexual attitudes and choices are strongly affected by the depth and breadth of adolescents' religious involvement:[18]

• 3% of the most religiously involved students said they believed it's okay for teenagers to have sex if they're emotionally ready for sex, compared with 56% of the least religiously involved.

• 18% of the most religiously involved students said they'd ever willingly touched or been touched by another person in private areas under their clothes, compared with 53% of the least religiously involved.

• 11% of the most religiously involved students said they'd had oral sex, compared with 30% of the least religiously involved.

• 9% of the most religiously involved students said they'd had sexual intercourse, compared with 26% of the least religiously involved.

• Among sexually active students, the most religiously involved reported an average of 2.7 sexual intercourse partners, compared with 4.1 partners reported by the least religiously involved.

Q: Are you at all surprised by the difference in the sexual attitudes and choices expressed by more and less religiously involved adolescents?

• Why do you think that difference exists?

• How would that explain "exceptions to the rule"? (For example, we've all known people who used youth group like a singles bar, and others who were very chaste in their relationships but wouldn't darken the door of the "youth room" under any circumstances).

Oral Sex[19]

• A 2003 report found that 20% of teenagers had three to four oral sex partners, compared to 8% of teenagers who had three to four sexual intercourse partners.

• A 2005 report found that boys engaged in oral sex at a younger age than girls; boys engaged when they were just over 13 years old, while girls engaged a year older, when they were just over 14.

• In a 2006 report, ninth graders who'd had oral sex gave their top six reasons for doing so (listed in order of the most-common reasons): improve relationship, pleasure, curiosity, peer pressure, fear, wants to.

• A 2003 report found that approximately one-third of teenagers said they'd engaged in oral sex, but one-fifth of teenagers didn't know that sexually transmitted diseases can be transmitted through oral sex.

RESPONSIBILITY

Session 6

THE BIG IDEA

Like it or not, we're all responsible for our own sexual behavior. Acting as if that were true—actually taking responsibility—is what this section is about.

Sexual responsibility is a bit like following the rules of the road. Every state has some version of the Basic Speed Law, which states that motorists may drive only as fast as is reasonable under prevailing conditions. That means drivers must slow down on wet or slippery pavement, regardless of the posted speed limit, and no matter what others do. "Everyone else was driving 65!" is interesting but not fascinating if you skid into another car on a slick highway. You still get the moving violation. If you're lucky, that's all you get.

"Everybody does it!" is no excuse for behavior that violates the basic speed law of sexuality. You're not responsible for "everybody"—whatever they may be up to—but you are responsible for your sexual choices.

It's not hard to understand sexual responsibility. Just ask yourself, *What are the prevailing conditions of my life?* And then ask, *Given those conditions, what is responsible sexual behavior?*

"Yeah, but you don't understand my situation. I'm not a slut or anything, but…I don't know, maybe I'm just hornier than most people."

That's an interesting theory; but if someone gets hurt, you're responsible for your behavior.

"No, but you don't understand. My girlfriend is really hot. I can't control myself."

Sorry, but if you lose control, that means you're driving too fast for prevailing conditions.

"But seriously, I think about sex all the time. That is my prevailing condition. Why would God give me hormonal surges and then tell me not to fulfill them? That's just mean."

It's not mean; it's a measure of human responsibility. If we were just like the other animals, things would be different. We're not. Humans have the capacity to live above our basic instincts, to live sacrificially, to live heroically.

"Fine, I'm responsible. Tell me to whom and for what, and I'll give it a shot."

Fair enough.

• We're responsible to God because God made us, and we belong to God before we belong to ourselves or anyone else.

• We're responsible to each other because we're brothers and sisters before we're anything else on the earth.

• We're responsible to ourselves because, even if we don't understand it, that inexpressible longing we feel is the longing to become what God made us to become.

The apostle Paul speaks:
> It is God's will that you should be sanctified: that you should avoid sexual immorality; that each of you should learn to control your own body in a way that is holy and honorable, not in passionate lust like the pagans, who do not know God; and that in this matter no one should wrong or take advantage of a brother or sister. The Lord will punish all those who commit such sins, as we told you and warned you before. For God did not call us to be impure, but to live a holy life.

> — 1 Thessalonians 4:3-7

Paul's definition of *sanctification* here is avoiding sexual immorality, learning to control our bodies in a way that's holy and honorable, and doing no harm to our sisters and brothers. You may not have to look outside your own youth group to see out-of-control people taking advantage of their brothers or sisters in Christ. Pity.

Paul spins it another way in a letter to the church at Rome:

Let us behave decently, as in the daytime, not in carousing and drunkenness, not in sexual immorality and debauchery, not in dissension and jealousy. Rather, clothe yourselves with the Lord Jesus Christ, and do not think about how to gratify the desires of the sinful nature.

— Romans 13:13-14

It's a vivid image. People who clothe themselves with the Lord Jesus Christ have a fighting chance at thinking about more than just how to gratify their own desires. For people who aren't clothed with Jesus, that's an uphill battle.

A lot of people lose that fight just about every day. Maybe you're one of them. Maybe you live in an endless spiral of determination, failure, resolution, failure, recommitment, failure, remorse, failure... All because you think clothing yourself with the Lord Jesus Christ means asking, What would Jesus do? and then attempting to behave as decently as you can—which, it turns out, is not all that decent. It's not that you're worse than other people; it's just that Jesus didn't so much ask us to do what he would do as say, "Apart from me you can do nothing" (John 15:5). It takes more than good intentions to power good behavior; it takes the power of Christ.

If you're going to win the fight, your only hope is to ask Jesus to help you win it. That takes a more thorough conversion than some of us have yet experienced.

But then people like us also need to ask others to help. Along with a deepening intimacy with the God who alone can sanctify and make us holy, acting responsibly takes support and accountability in the community of God's people.

NEW | The King and I

Read 2 Samuel 11–12.

Q: Is there any hint of David in you? Reflect upon that a bit.

• You probably haven't had anybody killed (if you have, maybe you should take that up with your youth worker before you go to bed tonight). But have you taken what wasn't yours to take sexually? Reflect on that a bit.

Q: Think for a moment—has God already sent Nathan to you in one form or another?

• If so, what happened?

• Could Nathan be in the wings, waiting for the right moment to tell you a story?

Look at Matthew 5:27-28.

Q: How, if at all, does this passage speak to your situation today?

Write a letter to God about the condition of your heart. What do you need God to do for you now that you can't do for yourself?

Q: Is there a Christian you know who's in sexual trouble?

• If so, do you think there's any chance God may want you to play the part of Nathan for that person?

• What would you do to make sure you acted like Nathan and stuck by the person instead of leaving once you've dropped the bad news?

Q: Do you know someone who doesn't follow Jesus who's in sexual trouble?

Look at 1 Corinthians 5:9-12.

• What does this suggest to you about how to approach a non-Christian who's sexually active?

• Is that person held to the same standard as a Christian? Why?

• Verse 12 suggests it's none of our business to judge people outside the church. Is that the same as not caring what your non-Christian friends do? Why or why not?

• What things can you say to express genuine, loving concern for non-Christian friends who are sexually active?

• What could keep you from doing that?

Write a letter to God about your hope for friends who are in sexual trouble. Ask God what he wants you to do to express love to them.

HOW I Junior

Take a few minutes and rate these people according to the following scale:
- 1—The person you'd be most likely to talk to about the issue listed (if you've ever struggled with it).
- 2—The person you'd be second most likely to talk to about the issue listed.
- 3—The person you can't imagine talking to about the issue under any circumstances.

	Mom or Stepmom	Dad or Stepdad	Sibling	Grandparent	Cousin	Aunt or Uncle	Neighbor	Friend	Teacher	Pastor	Youth Pastor	Therapist	Online Acquaintance
Compulsive Masturbation													
Pornography													
Sexual Fetish													
Pregnancy													
Peeping Tom Voyeurism													
Nonstop Fantasizing													
Sexual Harassment													
Rape													
Sexual Abuse													
Irresponsible Flirting													

Q: What do the 1s, 2s, and 3s in the chart tell you?

Q: If you're as sick as your secrets, how sick are you?
☐ Nearly dead because...

☐ I've been better because...

☐ Couldn't be better because...

Q: Think back a year. Compared to then, how would you say you're doing these days?
☐ Much better because…

☐ About the same because…

☐ Falling apart because…

• What do you think would have to happen for you to be much better a year from now?

• Do you believe you have what it takes to be much better? If not, do you think you know where to get it?

In the frame that follows, write or draw or encode the secret that makes you sickest.

• What does it cost you emotionally, spiritually, and relationally to keep that secret?

• Can you afford to keep paying that price?

Q: What do you think it would cost you to let someone in on your secret?

• Which looks like the bigger price—keeping the secret or letting it go? Why?

NOW | Line Up

Q: Which people have the greatest influence on you? How do they influence you?

Q: Which people have the greatest influence on your sexual attitudes and behaviors?

• Describe their influence—
☐ Positive because…

☐ Neutral because…

☐ Negative because…

Q: In several scientific studies, peer pressure has been identified as a major force in adolescent sexual behavior. How does your own experience confirm or contradict this?

• What kind of influence do you think you have on others' sexual behaviors and attitudes?
☐ Positive because…

☐ Neutral because…

☐ Negative because…

• Why do you think that's true?

• How do you feel about that influence?

Q: Is there anything you wish you could change about the way others influence your sexual attitudes and behaviors? If so, what would that be?

• Why would you like to change that?

• Is there someone who can support you in that wish?

Q: Is there anything you'd like to change about the way you influence other people's sexual attitudes and behaviors? If so, what would that be?

• Why is that important to you?

• Is there someone who can support you in that wish?

• How would you describe your desire for change if God happened to be listening right now (which, by the way, is the case)?

NOW | This Is a Test

You'll find the answers (as of this writing) on page 163.

1. What percent of Americans with a sexually transmitted infection are under the age of 25?

2. What percent of Americans will have a sexually transmitted infection at some point in their lifetimes?

3. What percent of sexually active people contract an STD by age 24?

4. Based on the 50 million adults who have herpes and the new infections diagnosed annually, what percent of Americans might have herpes by 2025?

5. What percent of infertile American women can attribute their infertility to tubal damage caused by pelvic inflammatory disease (PIV), the result of an untreated sexually transmitted disease?

6. What percent of adults ages 18 to 44 has ever been tested for a sexually transmitted disease or infection other than HIV/AIDS?

7. What percent of new AIDS diagnoses in the United States each year are women?

8. What percent of new HIV cases occurs among people under the age of 25?

9. What percent of those in the United States infected with HIV don't know it?

Q: Do you know anyone who you fear may be infected by a sexually transmitted disease? If so, why do you think that may be true?

• How did you come to possess that knowledge?

• Knowing what you know, what are your options?

• Do you believe that person might go for a blood test if you offered to go along? Why?

Q: If you've been sexually active, how do you know you're not infected?

• Have you been tested since your last sexual contact?

• What do you have to gain or lose by getting a blood test?

• What do you have to gain or lose by not getting a blood test?

Q: What is your responsibility to yourself and others when it comes to infectious diseases? Why?

NEW | Roe v. Wade

Q: Describe your emotional reaction to the word *abortion*.

• Why do you think you feel that way?

Q: How do you think your views on abortion compare with those of people at your school?

• How do your views compare with those of people at your church or youth group?

Q: Maybe you've thought about having an abortion, maybe you've had one, maybe you know someone who has. Whatever the case, how has your own life been affected by the issue of abortion?

Q: Do you think you have any responsibility to act regarding abortion? If so, what do you think you should do? Why?

• How does your sense of responsibility to God, or before God, affect your answer? If you're not sure, then you might want to check out Exodus 23:7; Psalm 139:13-16; or Proverbs 6:16-17. On a related note, Job 3 and Jeremiah 20:14-18 give voice to the despair some people feel about life.

• What do you have to gain or lose by acting on your belief about abortion?

NEW | The Home Front

Q: How would you describe your relationship with your parents?

• Think back through the past year. Would you say your relationship seems better, worse, or about the same? Why?

• How do you think your parents would answer that question? Why?

Q: How comfortable do you feel about talking with your parents about dating, love, or sex?
☐ Completely comfortable because…

☐ It depends because…

☐ Completely uncomfortable because…

• How comfortable do you think your parents are talking with you about dating, love, or sex?
☐ Completely comfortable because…

☐ It depends because…

☐ Completely uncomfortable because…

Read Exodus 20:12 and Ephesians 6:1-4.

Q: Based on Exodus 20:12 and Ephesians 6:1-4, what do you think it means to act responsibly and honor your parents in the middle of what you're experiencing romantically and sexually?

• How do you feel about that?

• Do you think there's anything you need to do differently in the way you relate to your parents?

HOW | Stopping Short

Here's what I wish I could take back...

I wish I could take back the silence. I wish I could take back my fear of asking the next question.

Demond and Chrissy had been dating for a while. Both were Christians, and both were friends of mine since we went to the same youth group. Chrissy also went to my school, and we were on the same step team, so I actually got to know her pretty well.

One day while Chrissy and I were riding home from step practice, she started talking about how much she was looking forward to going out with Demond that night. They hadn't seen each other in four days, and she was really missing him.

I asked, "So you and Demond are doing pretty well, huh?"

Chrissy paused a bit longer than I expected. "Yeah, I guess so."

She paused. (I didn't imagine it; she definitely paused. Should I ask why? Or should I just let it go? I knew her well enough now, so I decided to ask.)

"What do you mean you guess so?"

Chrissy looked out the car window as if she were wondering how much to say. "We're doing more physically than I thought we would."

We pulled up to a stoplight. Neither one of us spoke. It was like we weren't sure where the conversation should go.

She'd apparently decided. "But it's okay. I really like him, and he really likes me. It's not like we're having sex or anything."

I sensed Chrissy wanted to switch subjects. I decided that was okay by me. I didn't know how to go any deeper, so I took the discussion toward the shallow end. "I'm sure you guys are fine." I paused for a second and then diverted the conversation. "I'm so tired of our step coach. It's like she thinks we don't have a life outside of step. I can't wait until summer."

Q: What did the narrator in the story do well?

• Can you identify anything she could have done to be more helpful to her friend? If so, why do you think she didn't take it to the next level?

Q: When are you more likely to stop short:

☐ In asking my friends questions about their relationships, because…

☐ In volunteering information about my own issues and experiences, because…

Q: Do you think you have any responsibility to tell your story?

• Are there circumstances in which you think it might be unwise to tell your story? Write about that.

Q: If, as the old saying goes, "we're only as sick as our secrets," how much healthier could you get by disclosing your story appropriately?

• Is there someone you trust enough to share what's going on without stopping short? If not, would you be willing to ask God for such a friend?

• Where would you start looking for that person?

DO-OVERS

THE BIG IDEA

Sooner or later, everyone needs do-overs.

But can we get them?

Children learn about do-overs in friendly games of hopscotch and marbles. A do-over is a second chance when someone makes a mistake; it's a gift between friends. No one has a right to demand do-overs; no one can say, "Shut up, I'm taking a do-over." A do-over is a favor; an act of grace.

Grace is what this section is mainly about—do-overs for people who commit sexual fouls. Which is to say, all of us.

First, some bad news: for single people, young and old, sex is a high-risk behavior, like driving under the influence. If nothing goes wrong, maybe nobody gets hurt; if things go badly, maybe someone dies.

That worst-case scenario—someone dies—raises the stakes from, say, *lying*. Tell a lie and, if things go badly, the worst that usually happens (for you, at least) is you get caught and suffer the consequences of breaking trust—unpleasant, but endurable.

Getting caught sexually includes outcomes like pregnancy and sexually transmitted infections.

Getting caught sexually may also include unanticipated emotional consequences. There's an interesting idea in Paul's first letter to the Christians at Corinth: "Flee from sexual immorality," he says. "All other sins people commit are outside their bodies, but those who sin sexually sin against their own bodies" (1 Corinthians 6:18). Sex has an unusually personal effect because it's uniquely inside rather than outside us; sex isn't something we merely *do*...

This makes sense to anyone who's been surprised to find herself feeling shame about something she's done. Some people respond to that feeling by building up calluses where the pain is—like the tough spots on a tennis player's hands or a dancer's feet. But, eventually, a lot of people decide it's just not worth it and shut down their sexuality.

Which is too bad. Good sex is very good—it's not the meaning of life, but it's a good thing. It's sad when a bad impression of a good thing follows people into adulthood.

All of which begs the question: Can 16-year-old boys and girls burned-out on premature sex get do-overs? Our answer to that depends on how we answer another question: Is God *for* us or *against* us?

If God is against us, it's Game Over; there won't be any do-overs. We'll die forgiven but still guilty. Don't say God didn't warn us.

If, on the other hand, God is for us, there's hope. We still must contend with the natural consequences of our behavior, but as Betsie ten Boom (who didn't survive the Nazi concentration camps) told her sister Corrie (who did): "[We] must tell people what we have learned here. We must tell them that there is no pit so deep that He is not deeper still."[20]

For people who grew up hearing about the irreversible effects of sexual failure—how much worse it is than other wrongdoing—this is hard to believe. But if the Bible is true, *this* is true: God's forgiveness covers every kind of wrong. Because God is gracious, people like us get a chance to begin again, starting right where we are (even though it's not where we're supposed to be).

Just to be certain we've said it, let's embrace one lonely group of people who need do-overs in spite of themselves. They are the ones who were (or, God forbid, *are*) abused by their fathers, brothers, sisters, uncles, aunts, cousins, babysitters, teachers, pastors, and boyfriends. (If we've left out anyone, it's only because we can't bear to go on.)

These victims of sexualized violence tend to blame and punish themselves for what was done *to* them (not *by* them).

Hard as it may be to accept, this session points to the One who "heals the brokenhearted and binds up their wounds" (Psalm 147:3). If we do nothing else with do-overs, can we please offer sanctuary and hope to victims of sexual violence?

NEW | Clean or Unclean?

Compare Leviticus 20:9-22 with John 8:1-11.

Q: How do you feel about the tension between punishment and mercy for sexual wrongdoing?

• Where do you tend to come down on the scale?
☐ More toward punishment because...

☐ More toward tolerance because...

☐ More toward mercy because...

• Why do you think you've landed at that point on the scale?

• Looking at your own life and faith, where do you think God stands on the scale between punishment and mercy? What makes you think that?

Q: Do you know anyone who's really in need of God's mercy because of sexual wrongdoing?

• If so, why do you think this person needs mercy?

Q: Do you know anyone who needs to show mercy for sexual wrongdoing?

• If so, why do you think she needs to show mercy?

• What do you think it would cost that person to show mercy?

• What do you think she has to gain by showing mercy?

HOW I Who Me?

One of Hemingway's stories begins like this:

> Madrid is full of boys named Paco, which is the diminutive of the name Francisco, and there is a Madrid joke about a father who came to Madrid and inserted an advertisement in the personal columns of *El Liberal* which said: PACO MEET ME AT HOTEL MONTANA NOON TUESDAY ALL IS FORGIVEN PAPA and how a squadron of Guardia Civil had to be called out to disperse the eight hundred young men who answered the advertisement.[21]

Q: Hemingway's narrator describes the "all is forgiven" story as a joke. Does it sound funny to you?

Consider these stories…

STORY ONE I LUKE

I guess it all started when I was about 12. My older brother got a copy of a porno magazine and hid it under his bed. One day I was searching for something, and I found it—it wasn't very well hidden. I'd never seen anything like that in my life, and I was blown away that women would allow themselves to be photographed in positions like that.

It started slowly at first; I'd sneak into his room and just slowly go through all the pictures. I was a little grossed out in the beginning; but the more I looked at the magazine, the more attractive it became to me. I can't really remember when it happened first, but I sure can remember how good it felt. Masturbating felt so good that all I could think about all day at school was getting home to do it again. Here I am 12 years old, and I'm obsessed with these sexual feelings. Man they felt good.

I guess when I was about 14, those urges to masturbate got stronger and stronger. I remember once, while on a youth group trip to the beach, those feelings got so strong that I had to literally run into the bushes. At this point in my life, I was masturbating sometimes up to four or five times a day—talk about a problem.

I'm 20 now. For about six years, I've been seeking a solution to this problem, but nothing seems to get better. My stack of porno is so high, I can barely see over it. There's a nude beach about 50 miles away from where I live, and I spend most weekends down there taking pictures when the ladies aren't looking.

I hate what I do and who I am, but something just drives me to do this. I need help so bad; in fact, I wish I could just start all over again.

Q: If you'd known each other, where along the way might you have said, "Luke, let's do something else right now"?

• On a scale of 1 (hardly any) to 10 (a ton), how much help is that for Luke right now?

Q: Luke just came clean with this story. What do you want him to know first?

• What else do you want Luke to know?

• Anything else?

Q: What do you think "Go now and leave your life of sin" means for Luke?

• From the sound of Luke's account, how easy do you think it will be for him to hear these words of Jesus for himself?

• If you were Luke's friend, what could you do to help him go and leave his life of sin?

STORY TWO I MEGAN

This is so hard to talk about. I've never shared this with anyone before—it just makes me feel so dirty and abused. You'll have to bear with me…

We were such a close family. I used to stay over at my cousin's place as much as my own. My uncle seemed like another father to me. Our families did everything together—vacations, road trips, BBQs…you name it. We loved each other so much.

That is, until my 15th birthday. How could I ever forget it? I'd planned to spend this special night at my cousin's house; we were going to do a sleepover like we'd done so many times before. My cousin fell asleep way too quickly that night. I was a little bored, so I went downstairs to watch a bit of TV.

This is the tough part. From seemingly nowhere, my uncle appeared in the TV room and sat down beside me. I gave him a big hug as he wished me another happy birthday. What he gave me was the worst birthday anyone could ever have. I don't need to go into the details, do I? I suppose you can imagine what happened next. I tried to scream, but he told me he'd tell everyone that I forced him to do it to me. Somehow back then it made sense...so I did nothing.

He's in jail now. I came to my senses pretty quickly, and I told my mom what happened. No one believed me at first. Perhaps that was one of the worst things about the whole situation. I can remember overhearing discussions my parents had about the possibility of me making this up. That really hurt. No one really believed me until my cousin stepped up and said this had been happening to her for years.

My uncle says he's all sorry and everything and that he really found Jesus in prison. As far as I'm concerned, that's between him and Jesus.

It's been seven years since that night. I've never had a boyfriend and...truth be told, I hate men. A man just has to put his hand on my shoulder and I feel filthy—all I can think about whenever a man approaches me is my 15th birthday. It wasn't very happy.

Q: Megan just told you this story. What do you want her to know first?

• What else do you want Megan to know?

• Anything else?

Q: Why do you think Megan feels dirty?

Q: Megan was the victim—is there any sense in which she may still need do-overs?

• If so, how would her do-over be different from the one her uncle needs?

• If you don't think Megan needs a do-over, what does she need to get a fresh start after all this time?

Q: If you were Megan's friend, what could you do to help her keep going forward?

Q: What do you imagine Jesus saying to Megan?

STORY THREE | TAYLOR

It happened so fast. He was my boyfriend for only a few weeks when we went on a special date. After dinner and a movie, we went up to this place he knew about. We were having such a good night, and everything seemed to be going so well.

He parked the car, and we could see the city lights spread out below us like a blanket. Believe me, romance was in the air. We started to make out a little, just gentle kissing really. As our kissing became more enthusiastic, I could tell he was becoming very excited. Don't tell anyone, but I was, too.

He started to slip his hand under my blouse, and I tried to pull back. I'd never had anyone touch me there before. My head was screaming at me to stop him from doing this, but my body was screaming just as loud to let it keep happening. Before I even knew what was happening, his other hand was up my skirt, grabbing, and I knew it just had to stop.

I told him to stop, then I pushed him away with all my strength and tried to get out of the car. But he climbed on top of me and locked the door. Before I knew it, my skirt was lifted way up, and he was pushing my underwear down to my knees. I couldn't get my arms free; he was way too strong for me.

It was over nearly as soon as it began. I pushed him away, and I was so angry. But you know what? I was a lot angrier with myself. Maybe I shouldn't have worn that skirt. Maybe Mom was right—it sent the wrong signal. And I did let him touch my breast, so...

That was about a month ago. He hasn't talked to me since, and I never told anyone. There's no way that was rape. How could it be if there was even a small part of me that wanted it to happen? I just can't believe I lost my virginity that way. I just feel...I mean, truly, there's nothing to stop me having sex with anyone I'm attracted to now, right? It's not like I can undo that night.

Q: Taylor just told you this story. What do you want her to know first?

• What else do you want Taylor to know?

• Anything else?

Q: Taylor is angrier at herself than the boy who assaulted her. What's that about?

• She blames herself for what happened. Do you? Write about that.

Q: You're the first person she's told; who else needs to know?

Carl Jung wrote:
> That I feed the hungry, that I forgive an insult, that I love my enemy in the name of Christ—all these are undoubtedly great virtues. What I do unto the least of my brethren, that I do unto Christ. But what if I should discover that the least amongst them all, the poorest of all the beggars, the most impudent of all the offenders, the very enemy himself—that these are within me, and that I myself stand in need of the alms of my own kindness—that I myself am the enemy who must be loved—what then?[22]

Q: What would you say to Taylor about forgiving herself?

• What would you say is the difference between truly forgiving yourself and simply letting yourself off the hook?

Q: What's the most significant thing you're taking away from these stories?

• Why is that significant to you?

• What kind of help do you think you could use to follow through?

For more on dealing with sexual abuse and other tough stuff, see pages 159-161.

NEW | Scarlet Lady

Read Joshua 2:1-21; Joshua 6:20-25; Hebrews 11:31; and James 2:25, then write a "Once upon a time..." story about Rahab, including what you take to be the moral of the story.

Q: Why do you think God works with people like Rahab? Why not stick to virtuous Queen Esther or Joan of Arc types?

Q: What does the biblical record of Rahab's life suggest to you about God?

• Why do you think that message stands out for you?

Q: Are there any ways in which you're like Rahab? Write about that.

• Are there ways in which God has treated you like he treated Rahab? Write about that.

Q: If the story of Rahab demonstrates how God's accepts people, what do you want to do in response?

NEW | A Moveable Feast

Read Luke 7:36-50, then reflect on these questions.

Q: What do you think is the most important thing in this story? Why do you think it's important?

Q: With whom do you identify in this story?
☐ Simon the Pharisee because...

☐ The woman because...

☐ Jesus because...

☐ The other guests because...

Q: Do you think a person has to be a hooker* to appreciate how much she's been forgiven?

Q: How do you think you do at treating people as if Jesus was really serious about this?
☐ Not well at all because...

☐ I could do better because...

☐ I do pretty well most of the time because...

• How well do you do at treating yourself as if Jesus were really serious about this?
☐ Not well at all because...

☐ I could do better because...

☐ I do pretty well most of the time because...

* We don't know beyond a shadow and doubt that the unnamed woman in Luke 7:37 was a prostitute—only that Luke described the actions of "a woman in that town who had lived a sinful life..." William Barclay represents the woman as a notorious sinner in his commentary on Luke: "The woman was a bad woman, and a notoriously bad woman, a prostitute." John Gill's exposition on Luke also calls the woman "a notorious sinner...; a lewd woman, a vile prostitute, a harlot" and adds the original language "signifies both a sinner and a whore" (citing Castell. Lex. Heptaglott. col. 1195). Some have leapt to the conclusion that this story refers to Mary Magdalene, but that possibility seems unlikely since Mary is introduced by name later in Luke 8.

Q: What do you think you may have yet to learn from this story?

• What do you imagine you have to gain or lose by learning that lesson?

• Write a note to God about that.

NEW | Calling Your Bluff

Read John 4:1-42, then reflect on these questions.

Q: What stands out for you in this story? Why is that significant to you?

Q: What do you have in common with this woman?

• How are you different?

Q: Would you consider what you've done (or failed to do) to be any worse (or better) than the woman in this story? Write about that.

• Write about how you may be able to use your story of failure to introduce people to Jesus.

Q: What do you think you have to gain or lose by using your failure story to introduce people to Jesus?

• Is it worth it? Why or why not?

NEW | Falling...and Bouncing Back

Read Psalms 32 and 51.

Q: What stands out for you in these passages?

• Why do you think that strikes you?

• With which lines do you most closely identify? Because...

Q: In what ways do you think you're least like David?

See if you can write a poem or draw a picture that describes how you feel about God's intervention in your most significant failure.

Q: Have you yet made the kind of recovery from your most significant failure that David made in his? Write about that.

• What did you do—or what do you think you still need to do—to have that kind of recovery?

Write a prayer asking God to come to your aid as he helped David.

NEW | You Want Me to Marry a What?

Read Hosea 1–3, then reflect on these questions.

Q: How do you respond to the story of Hosea?

Q: With whom do you identify most?
☐ Hosea because…

☐ Gomer because…

☐ God because…

☐ The people whose attention God was trying to get, because…

Q: If you'd been Hosea's friend and he told you what God was asking him to do, what would you have told him? Why?

• If you were Gomer's friend and she told you she was going to marry the prophet, what would you have told her?

Q: The prophets sometimes seem like God's stuntmen, doing outlandish things to make in-your-face examples for people who didn't seem to get the picture. Has God done anything spectacular to get your attention?

Q: Do you know anyone who could stand to hear the story of Hosea and Gomer (and God and his people)?

• If so, what makes you think that person needs to hear this story? What do you think you can do about that?

HOW | Picture This

An old preacher said, "You will know the truth, and the truth will make you flinch before it sets you free."

Q: Have you been flinching about the truth of your sexuality? Write about that.

Q: How close to being sexually free would you say you are right now?
☐ Pretty much there because…

☐ Well on my way because…

☐ Not even close because…

Q: What do you think it will take to get you where God created you to be?

• Besides God, who else do you think can help?

• What do you think you want to do about all that?

• Is there anything keeping you from it?

THE STUFF AT THE BACK OF THE BOOK

Plumbing + Wiring FAQs

Don't hate us. We didn't ask the questions; we're just trying to respond honestly. So skip the ones you think are obvious and be glad there's somebody out there who knows less than you. At the end of every answer, feel free to circle whether you knew it or didn't know it.

Q: Is there a right way to kiss?

Uh, lip-to-lip works pretty well. The truth is that kissing comes pretty naturally for most people, and the rest catch on with a little practice. We found the back of the hand, pressing the thumb against the first finger, is a reasonably good place to work on technique...just kidding...okay we really did that, but only a couple of times, and never in front of a mirror. Sometimes noses get bumped and braces get locked up, but those mishaps are rare.
Knew it/Didn't know it

Q: How do people breathe when they kiss?

Although the mouth is pretty preoccupied during kissing, the nose usually isn't—nor should it be—making kissing more difficult, but not impossible, during the cold and flu season.
Knew it/Didn't know it

Q: What exactly happens during sex?

Technically, the sexual act proceeds through several phases. The first is an excitement phase, marked by an increase in pulse and blood pressure as blood rushes to the surface of the body. Genital fluids are also secreted during the excitement phase (for both the guy and girl), and the vagina expands (that would be the girl only—just to clarify). The next phase is the plateau phase, which is pretty brief and may conclude with an orgasm. The third phase is the resolution phase, during which the girl's and the guy's bodies return to normal.
Knew it/Didn't know it

Q: What's an orgasm?

An orgasm, also called a climax, is the peak of physical sexual excitement and gratification. Physically, it's marked by a faster pulse, higher blood pressure, intensely pleasurable sensations in the genitalia, and spasms of the pelvic muscles that cause contractions in the girl's vagina and sperm ejaculation from the guy's penis. Emotionally, it's marked by an overwhelming feeling of pleasure and release. Depending on who you're having sex with, it might also be a guilty pleasure—a mix of "I can't believe how good that felt" and "I can't believe how bad I feel about how good that felt." **Knew it/Didn't know it**

Q: Does an orgasm always happen during intercourse?

Not always. Sometimes the guy and girl feel fairly aroused together, but neither (or only one) will actually have an orgasm. It's also possible to have an orgasm before or after sexual intercourse. **Knew it/Didn't know it**

Q: Is an orgasm different for a guy than for a girl?

Well, yes, because they have different body parts. Both experience quick, rapid muscular contractions, but the girl's usually lasts longer. The girl also can have several orgasms, one right after another, while the guy usually has to wait awhile (like several hours). However, since the guy usually becomes aroused more quickly, he has orgasms more consistently during sexual intercourse. **Knew it/Didn't know it**

> I used to think I'd just want to have sex 24 hours a day. I didn't know that the body parts just get tired and sore after a while. I didn't know that sometimes I'd just be too tired to care about it and just want to go to sleep.
> —Hanna, on the information she got about sex

Q: Do orgasms always feel the same?

No. They're almost always good, but sometimes they're really great. Often how great it is relates to how connected you're feeling to your partner, how physically fresh and aroused you are, how mentally focused or distracted you are, and how emotionally free you feel to enjoy what's going on. *Knew it/Didn't know it*

Q: How long does an orgasm take?

Although the orgasm is the most talked about phase in sexual intercourse, it's actually pretty short, ranging from five to 30 seconds. *Knew it/Didn't know it*

Q: What's an erection?

When a guy becomes sexually aroused by physical or psychological stimulation, the blood flowing into his penis is increased, and the blood flowing out of his penis is temporarily reduced. As a result, the tissue swells and the penis is enlarged, hardened, and elevated. *Knew it/Didn't know it*

Q: I've heard that alcohol will help your sex drive, but I've also heard it will hurt it. What's the deal?

Alcohol is a depressant, so it tends to reduce inhibitions and dull decision-making skills. So people who've had something to drink may be more flirtatious or willing to try things they wouldn't even consider when they were sober. Because of this, some people jump to the conclusion that alcohol increases sex drive. But actually, alcohol depresses the nervous system and diminishes muscular coordination and nerve sensation. Sober sex is generally more pleasurable than sex under the influence. Perhaps the biggest gotcha is that the risk of pregnancy and sexually transmitted infections is increased by carelessness, so reread the first sentence and do the math. *Knew it/Didn't know it*

Q: Does sex hurt?

Vaginal sex can be painful—especially the first few times, and especially for women. Imagine going dancing for the first time. Since you don't know what you're doing and you haven't practiced, you might hurt yourself or your partner. The same is true for sex when you're new at it. This is one reason why "wham, bam, thank you ma'am" encounters are generally disappointing for women, while the patient, caring, unhurried touch of someone who's not in a rush because you're married for life can make the experience go more smoothly right from the start. *Knew it/Didn't know it*

Anal penetration is another thing altogether, and it can be quite painful. Unlike the vagina, the anus isn't very elastic, doesn't secrete sexual fluids to lubricate the opening, and is more subject to abrasions and tearing (not weeping; small rips in the tissue). Abrasions and tears make anal penetration far more risky than vaginal sex for the transmission of bacterial and viral diseases. ***Knew it/Didn't know it***

Q: Does the size of a penis matter?

Most guys assume the average size of an erect penis is six inches, and then they get worried because theirs is smaller than that. However, the reality is that an erect penis is usually around 5.1 or 5.2 inches, and a non-erect (or flaccid) penis is 3.5 inches. Regardless of penis size, a guy really doesn't need to worry about it. In a miracle of creative design, the girl's body adjusts to fit whatever size he is. ***Knew it/Didn't know it***

Q: Is masturbation wrong?

Ah, that's a biggie. Masturbation, or stimulating your own genitals for pleasure, has both fans and critics. Some people believe it's wrong all the time, others believe it's right almost all of the time, and still others fall somewhere in the middle, arguing that occasional masturbation is okay, as long as it isn't fueled by lustful fantasies and doesn't become a disruptive, self-absorbed preoccupation (which happens to more people than you might think—or maybe it happens to fewer people than you might think—depending on what you might think). We fall somewhere in the middle. For more about masturbation, see Section 4, "Desire."
Knew it/Didn't know it

Q: What is oral sex?

Contrary to early reports, oral sex is not talking about sex. Who knew? Instead, it means using the mouth to stimulate another person's genital organs. Also contrary to early reports, sexual infections are transmitted fairly easily through cuts, abrasions, tears, and sores in and around the mouth. ***Knew it/Didn't know it***

Q: Is oral sex the same as sex?

Well, babies can't be conceived during oral sex, if that's what you're asking. But we're inclined to say that anything that includes the word sex—vaginal sex, anal sex, oral sex—is sex. And don't think that dropping the word sex—"Oh we only do oral," or "I only do anal"—changes the substance of the behavior. The exchange of body fluids is a pretty reliable clue. Sexual gratification is another clue. As one of our friends admitted after breaking off a relationship with a married person who kept offering assurances that they weren't really having sex: "No, we didn't have intercourse...but an orgasm is an orgasm, so..." We didn't know about the affair until it was over and our friend was trying to make amends—hoping for do-overs from an emotionally damaging mistake. ***Knew it/Didn't know it***

Q: What if my breasts are different sizes?

That's just how some girls are. There's nothing wrong with it, especially when your breasts are still developing; however, if you notice any lumps in them, you should have a medical doctor look at them just to make sure it's not a tumor or a cyst. ***Knew it/Didn't know it***

Q: What if my testicles are different sizes?

That's just how some guys are. If the larger testicle is hard, a guy should have it checked out by a medical doctor to make sure it's not a cyst, tumor, or hernia. ***Knew it/Didn't know it***

Q: What are wet dreams, and why do they happen?

Wet dreams are also known as nocturnal emissions. Starting at puberty, as a guy's body begins to mature, he's likely to have involuntary emissions of semen from his penis during sleep. Nocturnal emissions sometimes accompany sexually stimulating dreams—hence the term *wet dream*. ***Knew it/Didn't know it***

Q: Have I done something wrong if I have a wet dream?

Some guys feel guilty about wet dreams—maybe because they remind them of when they used to wet the bed or maybe because they're dreaming about specific girls or women when the emissions occur. However, it's just a natural, subconscious event that doesn't necessarily mean anything. ***Knew it/Didn't know it***

Q: If the guy withdraws before he ejaculates, can the girl still get pregnant?

During extended foreplay a small amount of pre-ejaculatory fluid seeps from a guy's penis. This fluid contains real, live, and active sperm that can get the girl pregnant. Because of this, withdrawing the penis from the vagina before ejaculation is not generally considered reliable birth control. ***Knew it/Didn't know it***

Q: And what exactly is foreplay?

Foreplay is the early stage of sex that gets people ready for the main event. In other words, making out is foreplay. This explains why people get all worked up and frustrated when they make out—and why they're tempted to move on to the main event prematurely. ***Knew it/Didn't know it***

Q: I've heard that a girl won't get pregnant if she has sex standing up or if she has sex in a hot tub. Is that true?

The girl can be jumping up and down or doing handstands, cartwheels, or backflips. If the guy introduces sperm into her vagina, then she could get pregnant. The position doesn't matter and neither does her environment. She can be in a hot tub, sauna, submarine, or spacecraft—if she's having vaginal sex, then she could get pregnant at any time. **Knew it/Didn't know it**

Q: Does having sex change you physically?

The biggest change is that if you're a girl, you could get pregnant. Also for girls, a physical membrane called the hymen (a sheet-like lining just inside the vagina) can break, which might hurt and cause some bleeding. For guys nothing really changes physically. Either gender can pick up or pass along a sexually transmitted disease at any time (including the first time). Oh yeah, and did we mention that if you're a girl, you could get pregnant? We don't mean to harp, but that's a pretty huge change. **Knew it/Didn't know it**

Q: Why am I hearing so much now about the HPV vaccine. What is it? Should I get it?

Coming up with an answer to the first question isn't all that hard. In 2007, the U.S. Food and Drug Administration (FDA) released a vaccine developed to prevent cervical cancer and other diseases in females caused by certain types of human papillomavirus (HPV) transmitted by genital, anal, or oral contact. This vaccine (called Gardasil) protects against four types of HPV, which together create 70% of cervical cancers and 90% of genital warts.

The second question is trickier. The FDA licensed this vaccine for girls and women ages 9 to 26, and it's more effective before women become sexually active. Some folks believe that getting the vaccine might encourage premature sexual activity. Others believe it's important to get the vaccine even if you plan to remain abstinent because you might not live up to your plan, or there might be circumstances beyond your control—meaning sexual assault. Whether or not you get the vaccine is something you should talk over with your parents and other wise adults who know you well. **Knew it/Didn't know it**

Q: Will I get AIDS if I'm around someone who has it?

According to the U.S. Centers for Disease Control and Prevention, HIV (Human Immunodeficiency Virus, the virus that causes AIDS, or Acquired Immunodeficiency Syndrome) isn't transmitted through day-to-day activities such as shaking hands, hugging, or a casual kiss. Nor can you become infected from a toilet seat, drinking fountain, doorknob, dishes, food, or pets. HIV is primarily found in the blood, semen, or vaginal fluid of an infected person and can be transmitted by having sex (anal, vaginal, or oral), sharing contaminated needles, during pregnancy, or through breast-feeding. ***Knew it/Didn't know it***

Q: Sex is always neat and clean in the movies—is that right?

Sex is messy—not gross, necessarily, but messy. When the guy ejaculates, the two to six milliliters of semen containing about 300,000,000 sperm have to go somewhere. Plus the girl's vagina builds up additional lubrication. You figure it out. ***Knew it/Didn't know it***

Q: Christians are so prudish. They must have lousy sex, right?

Actually, quite the opposite, if a national survey of 3,500 Americans ages 18 to 59 is to be believed. According to this 1994 survey, Protestant Christian women are most likely to achieve orgasm each and every time they have vaginal intercourse. Could this be a fringe benefit of following Christ?[23] ***Knew it/Didn't know it***

Back-to-Basics Biology

This is a cheat sheet on basic sexual biology. Use it to refresh your memory from health class. (This won't be on the test.) Feel free to circle whether you knew it or didn't know it.

Clitoris—Apparently the only organ in the human anatomy designed solely for experiencing sexual stimuli, the female clitoris is a two- to three-centimeters long funnel loaded with nerve endings. It's very sensitive to both pleasure and pain. ***Knew it/Didn't know it***

Coronal ridge—The bulge near the end of the penis. ***Knew it/Didn't know it***

Glans (or head)—If a male has been circumcised, the glans (or head) is located at the end of the penis. If a male hasn't been circumcised, the glans is covered with a loose skin called the foreskin. ***Knew it/Didn't know it***

Labia majora—A part of the vulva that protects the rest of the vagina. If a female hasn't given birth, then the outer lips of the labia majora probably meet at the center of her genitals. ***Knew it/Didn't know it***

Ovaries—The ovaries are female internal organs shaped like large almonds. They're located on either side of the uterus and produce some of the sex hormones that affect the menstrual cycle. Their primary function, however, is to release one of about 400,000 eggs for reproduction 14 days before a girl's period begins. The egg is either fertilized by a guy's sperm and becomes implanted in the uterus, or it's discharged from the body with the menstrual blood flow. This process begins in puberty and continues until menopause. ***Knew it/Didn't know it***

Penis—The penis is the obvious external male organ for sexual intercourse and the method by which sperm is introduced into a female's vagina. During sexual excitement, blood is temporarily trapped in the chambers of the erectile tissue in the penis, causing the penis to become enlarged, firm, and erect. ***Knew it/Didn't know it***

Scrotum—A pouch in the male anatomy that holds two glands called the testes. ***Knew it/Didn't know it***

Seminal vesicles—Glands that secrete many of the components of semen into the vas deferens (keep reading to find out what a vas deferens is). ***Knew it/Didn't know it***

Shaft—The cylindrical structure of the penis. ***Knew it/Didn't know it***

Sperm—Cells from a male that are capable of fertilizing a mature egg in a female reproductive system. The process of sexual arousal and ejaculation activates the otherwise immobile cells so they become self-propelled in the seminal fluid by means of a tiny tail that whips from side to side. Sperm are available more or less on demand in quantities of around 300,000,000 cells per ejaculation. Under favorable conditions sperm live about three days after ejaculation. *Knew it/Didn't know it*

Testes—The testes (the primary male reproductive organ) are two small balls that move around in the scrotum and generate sperm. *Knew it/Didn't know it*

Uterus (also called the womb)—A pear-shaped muscular organ in the female reproductive system, located between the urinary bladder and rectum, that connects through the cervix to the vagina. The lining of the uterus—the endometrium—secretes fluids that keep eggs and sperm alive and nourishes fertilized eggs. If a mature egg isn't fertilized, then it's flushed out with the endometrium through the vagina during monthly menstruation. *Knew it/Didn't know it*

Urethra—The thin tube that carries urine from the male bladder—or sperm from the seminal vesicles—through the penis. *Knew it/Didn't know it*

Vagina—The vagina (the muscular canal leading from the vulva to the uterus) changes in size to receive any size penis during intercourse and expands to accommodate a baby during delivery. *Knew it/Didn't know it*

Vas deferens—The duct through which sperm moves from the testicles to the urethra. *Knew it/Didn't know it*

Vulva—The external female genitalia that surround the opening to the vagina. *Knew it/Didn't know it*

How to Help Victims of Sexual Abuse and Other Tough Stuff

If you start talking honestly with your friends, there's always the chance that someone will share something shocking. If a friend reveals things about her sexual experience that are troubling, frightening, or even dangerous, don't freak out. Chances are if someone chooses to trust you with a difficult story about sexual abuse, then she won't be going off the deep end any time soon. She's probably silently carried the story for a while already, and you've given her the impression you can help.

You can. You can't *solve* anything, but you can help her get the help she needs. So, take a deep breath, express your sympathy, and listen like crazy.

If, after you hear a friend's story, you believe that a reasonable person would call it sexual abuse, molestation, assault, or rape, chances are it is. If that's the case, the next step is help your friend find more help than you can probably offer on your own.

If you're not sure how to do that, and if your friend doesn't believe she (or he) can get real help at home, use one or more of these resources:

• If you're honestly afraid for someone's life, don't wait around and overthink it—dial 911 and explain that you believe your friend is an immediate danger to herself or to others. These are powerful words in any emergency response system: *I believe my friend is a danger to herself or to others.* Don't say these words if you don't mean them. And don't hesitate to say them if you believe they're true.

• Offer to go with your friend to see a trustworthy staff member in your church or youth group. That person will probably know what to do. If you're convinced the situation is real and if your youth leader seems confused or if you're afraid he'll sweep it under the rug, be sure you take the next steps.

• Take your friend to the head counselor or vice principal at your school—whoever on the staff or faculty seems to genuinely care about students. This person is what the law calls a "Mandated Reporter" (so is your youth leader, most likely, but you can be confident that school personnel have been down this road before). Mandated Reporters are obligated by law to report stories of sexual abuse that they believe to be true. Chances are the person you tell will call the sheriff, police, or Child Protective Services (or whatever that's called where you live). Law enforcement jurisdictions can be confusing, and it's easy to get lost along the way. School personnel have probably already been through this (more often than they wish)—they'll walk you through it.

• Get in touch with a trustworthy counselor or therapist and ask for her help. By the way, the counselor is a Mandated Reporter, too (as are your pastors and youth leaders though, unfortunately, they don't always know about that). Don't let the whole Mandated Reporter thing set you back. If your friend were going to solve this problem without outside help, she would have done so by now. So, unless you're a true expert on sex abuse recovery, it only makes sense to call on people who can protect and defend your friend. And, by the way, if you are a real expert, then you're a Mandated Reporter, too.

• If you go through all of these channels, and you believe nothing is happening, then start again at the top, humbly express your frustration, and ask for help. You're looking for justice in a system where you probably don't feel at home. That's okay. Keep after it. They'll listen to you eventually, if you don't give up.

• If you fear for a friend's safety and can't seem to get the help you need locally, call the **Boys Town Hotline: 800-448-3000**. Boys Town offers a full range of help to callers; they're very nice people, and they know what they're talking about.

• **800-4-A-CHILD** is the number for **Childhelp USA**. They specialize in sexual abuse assistance—also very nice and very helpful.

Then…

Stay close to your friend. Revealing the sordid details of an abusive relationship or sexual assault is a gruesome ordeal for almost anyone. In many cases these days, multidisciplinary intervention teams from Child Protective Services (CPS) are responsible for reducing the trauma kids suffer as a result of crimes against them. The CPS team is trained to tackle the legal, psychological, and family aspects of an investigation. The result is that kids are spared the agony of having to tell their horror story over and over again to a host of different people. But don't depend on that. Do what you can to remain close for the duration.

Be alert for signs of self-injurious behavior. Once they've told someone about abuse, it's not unusual for adolescents to enter a period of high risk for suicide, drug abuse, and other self-destructive behaviors. Families don't always respond the way we hope. Instead of surrounding the victim with loving concern, families sometimes respond in disbelief, anger, shock, or paralysis, leaving their child unsupported. Step into the gap as much as you can and get your friend to adults who can and will help.

Finally…

Bug your youth leaders to be prepared for hard times by picking up a copy of *The Youth Worker's Guide to Helping Teenagers in Crisis* (Rich Van Pelt and Jim Hancock, Youth Specialties, 2005). Tell them to pay special attention to the sections on Pregnancy, Incest, Sexual Abuse, Rape, Sexual Identity Issues, Self-Injurious Behavior, Eating Disorders, Sexual Abuse Reporting, and Referrals.

Loveline Answer Sheet

#1: Adam, 18 years old, calls in and says that when he was 16, he slept with his high school English teacher about 10 times. She got pregnant not long after and refused to have any more contact with him. He saw the baby recently and says it looks exactly like him. He's sure it's his, but he doesn't know what to do.

The *Loveline* hosts told Adam to stay out of the situation because he has absolutely nothing to offer this child. It's better if the child never knows who his father is. (And, no, if you're wondering, the first caller wasn't longtime *Loveline* cohost Adam Carolla.)

#2: Toni, a 25-year-old female transvestite, calls in to ask for some advice. She slept with a girlfriend's fiancé. The girlfriend has no idea that her future marriage partner is thinking about becoming a transvestite as well. Should Toni tell her friend what she knows?

The *Loveline* hosts told Toni to stay out of it and let the couple work it out themselves.

#3: Melissa, 19, says she was at a house with three male friends, when they spiked her drink with a speedball (part heroin, part cocaine). When she'd completely lost control of her senses, these three so-called friends gang-raped her. That was six months ago. Since then, Melissa has had compulsive sex with more than 30 men— all one-night stands. She doesn't know why she's doing this.

The *Loveline* hosts told Melissa she had a compulsive addiction to sex that had been triggered by this event. She was told to get counseling and connect with an AA-type group.

This Is a Test Fact Sheet

Q 1: What percent of Americans with a sexually transmitted infection are under the age of 25?
A: 50%, meaning half [24]

Q 2: What percent of Americans will have a sexually transmitted infection at some point in their lifetimes?
A: 50%, meaning half [25]

Q 3: What percent of sexually active people contract an STD by age 24?
A: 33% or one in three [26]

Q 4: Based on the 50 million adults who have herpes and the new infections diagnosed annually, what percent of Americans might have herpes by 2025?
A: 40% or two out of five [27]

Q 5: What percent of infertile American women can attribute their infertility to tubal damage caused by pelvic inflammatory disease (PIV), the result of an untreated sexually transmitted disease?
A: 15% or approximately one out of six [28]

Q 6: What percent of adults ages 18 to 44 have ever been tested for a sexually transmitted disease or infection other than HIV/AIDS?
A: Less than 50% or less than half [29]

Q 7: What percent of new AIDS diagnoses in the United States each year are women?
A: 27% or approximately one in four [30]

Q 8: What percent of new HIV cases occur among people under the age of 25?
A: 50% or half [31]

Q 9: What percent of those in the United States infected with HIV don't know it?
A: 24% to 27% or approximately one out of four [32]

All the Sex in the Bible

By Bible Passage

Genesis 1:28	reproduction
Genesis 2:24	one flesh
Genesis 4:1	Adam and Eve
Genesis 4:17	Cain and his wife
Genesis 16:1-16	Abraham, Sarah, and Hagar
Genesis 19:1-29	Sodom and Gomorrah
Genesis 19:30-35	Lot and his daughters
Genesis 29:21-30	Jacob, Leah, and Rachel
Genesis 34:1-31	Dinah's rape and rescue
Genesis 30:1-24	Leah and Rachel's maidservants and Jacob
Genesis 35:22	Reuben and his father's concubine
Genesis 38:1-30	Tamar and her in-laws
Genesis 39:1-21	Joseph and Potiphar's wife
Exodus 19:15	abstinence
Exodus 22:16	sleeping around
Exodus 22:19	sex with animals
Leviticus 15:16-17	wet dreams
Leviticus 15:18	sexual hygiene
Leviticus 15:19-28	sexual hygiene for females
Leviticus 18:6-13	incest
Leviticus 18:14-18	sleeping around
Leviticus 18:19	abstinence during a woman's period
Leviticus 18:20-21	sleeping around
Leviticus 18:22	homosexuality
Leviticus 18:23	sex with animals
Leviticus 18:24-30	consequences of sex acts listed in verses 6-23
Leviticus 19:20	sleeping around
Leviticus 19:29	prostitution in the family
Leviticus 20:10-12	consequences of sleeping around
Leviticus 20:13	consequences of homosexuality

Leviticus 20:15-16	consequences of sex with animals
Leviticus 20:17, 19-20	consequences of incest
Leviticus 20:18	abstinence during a woman's period
Leviticus 20:21	sex with in-laws
Leviticus 22:4	sexual hygiene for males
Numbers 5:11-31	handling suspicions about spouse's adultery
Numbers 25:1-3	spiritual side effect of sleeping around
Deuteronomy 22:13-21	divorce after consummation
Deuteronomy 22:22-24	consequences of sleeping around
Deuteronomy 22:25-29	consequences of rape
Deuteronomy 23:10-11	wet dreams
Deuteronomy 24:5	marital sex the first year
Deuteronomy 25:5-10	sex to carry on the family name
Deuteronomy 27:20	consequences of sleeping with a stepmother
Deuteronomy 27:21	consequences of bestiality
Deuteronomy 27:22	consequences of incest
Deuteronomy 27:23	consequences of sleeping with an in-law
Judges 16:1	Samson and a prostitute
Judges 16:4-20	Samson and Delilah
Judges 19:16-30	rape of a concubine
Ruth 4:13	Boaz and Ruth
1 Samuel 1:19-20	Elkanah and Hannah
1 Samuel 2:22	Eli's sons and the church women
2 Samuel 11:2-5	David and Bathsheba (first sexual encounter)
2 Samuel 11:11	Uriah and abstinence from marital sex
2 Samuel 12:11	Nathan's prophecy about David's concubines
2 Samuel 12:24	David and Bathsheba (marital sex)
2 Samuel 13:1-22	rape of Tamar
2 Samuel 16:20-22	Absalom and David's concubines
1 Chronicles 2:21	Hezron and the daughter of Makir
1 Chronicles 7:23	Ephraim and his wife

Proverbs 2:11-19	wisdom as a safeguard against seduction
Proverbs 5:1-20	dangers of sleeping around versus pleasures of married sex
Proverbs 6:20-35	wisdom as a safeguard against seduction
Proverbs 7:1-27	wisdom as a safeguard against seduction
Proverbs 23:26-28	warning about prostitutes
Song of Songs	romantic poetry of marital sex
Isaiah 8:3	Isaiah and his wife
Isaiah 57:5	lusting
Jeremiah 2:20	Israel compared to a prostitute
Jeremiah 3:1-20	allegorical sex escapades of Israel and Judah
Ezekiel 16:1-42	allegory of wife becoming prostitute
Ezekiel 23:1-49	allegory of two promiscuous sisters
Hosea 1:2	Hosea and adulterous wife
Hosea 2:2-15	allegorical lust and sleeping around
Hosea 3:1-3	Hosea buys back his wife after prostitution
Hosea 4:10-19	consequences of physical and spiritual prostitution
Hosea 8:9	metaphor of Israel as a prostitute
Hosea 9:1	metaphor of Israel as a prostitute
Nahum 3:4	metaphor of Assyria as a prostitute
Matthew 5:27-30	lust and adultery
Matthew 15:19	source of sexual sin
Matthew 19:5	becoming one flesh
Matthew 19:9	divorce and sleeping around
Mark 7:21	source of sexual sin
John 4:16	woman at the well
John 8:3-11	Jesus and the adulterous woman
Acts 15:20, 29	sexual sin
Acts 21:25	sexual sin

Romans 1:24-27	lust and homosexuality
Romans 13:13-14	safeguard against orgies and sexual sin
1 Corinthians 5:1-2	Paul's reaction to sexual sin
1 Corinthians 6:9-10	consequences of sleeping around, prostitution, and homosexuality
1 Corinthians 6:12-20	fleeing sexual sin and prostitutes
1 Corinthians 7:2-5	sexual gratification and abstinence in marriage
1 Corinthians 7:9	lust and staying single
1 Corinthians 10:8	consequences of sleeping around
2 Corinthians 12:21	Paul's reaction to sexual sin
Galatians 5:19-21	source and consequences of sexual sin
Ephesians 5:3	warning against sleeping around
Ephesians 5:31	husband and wife as one flesh
Colossians 3:5	warning against lust and sleeping around
1 Thessalonians 4:3-5	God's view of lust and sexual sin
James 1:13-15	metaphor of sin as seduction
Jude 1:7	example of Sodom and Gomorrah
Revelation 2:14	Balaam, Balak, and sexual sin
Revelation 2:20-22	allegorical sleeping around (for the church of Thyatira)
Revelation 9:21	sexual sin
Revelation 17:1-2	allegorical "great prostitute"
Revelation 18:2-3, 9	allegory of Babylon, the great prostitute
Revelation 19:1-2	allegory of Babylon, the great prostitute
Revelation 21:8	sexual sin and the lake of fire
Revelation 22:15	sexual sin and Christ's return

By Topic

abstinence
Exodus 19:15
1 Corinthians 7:2-5

allegorical sex
Jeremiah 2:20
Jeremiah 3:1-20
Ezekiel 16:1-42
Ezekiel 23:1-49
Hosea 2:2-15
Hosea 8:9
Hosea 9:1
Nahum 3:4
Ephesians 5:31
James 1:13-15
Revelation 2:20-22
Revelation 17:1-2
Revelation 18:2-3, 9
Revelation 19:1-2

ancient Hebrew sexual hygiene
Leviticus 15:16-28
Leviticus 18:19
Leviticus 20:18
Leviticus 22:4
Deuteronomy 23:10-11

consequences of sexual sin
Genesis 19:1-29
Exodus 22:16
Exodus 22:19
Leviticus 18:6-30
Leviticus 19:29
Leviticus 20:12-13, 15-22
Numbers 5:11-31
Numbers 25:1-3
Deuteronomy 22:13-29
Deuteronomy 27:20-23
Judges 16:4-20
Proverbs 2:11-19
Proverbs 5:1-14
Proverbs 6:20-35
Proverbs 7:1-27
Proverbs 23:26-28
Jeremiah 3:1-20
Ezekiel 16:1-42
Ezekiel 23:1-49
Hosea 2:2-15
Hosea 4:10-19
Matthew 5:27-30
Matthew 19:9
John 8:3-11
Romans 1:24-27
1 Corinthians 6:9-10
1 Corinthians 6:12-20
1 Corinthians 10:8
Galatians 5:19-21
Ephesians 5:3
Colossians 3:5
Jude 1:7
Revelation 21:8
Revelation 22:15

divorce
Deuteronomy 22:13-21
Matthew 19:9

having children

Genesis 1:28
Genesis 4:1
Genesis 4:17
Genesis 16:1-16
Genesis 19:30-35
Genesis 30:1-24
Genesis 38:1-30
Deuteronomy 25:5-10
Ruth 4:13
1 Samuel 1:19-20
2 Samuel 11:2-5
2 Samuel 12:24
1 Chronicles 2:21
1 Chronicles 7:23
Isaiah 8:3

homosexuality

Leviticus 18:22
Leviticus 20:13
Romans 1:24-27
1 Corinthians 6:9-10

incest

Genesis 19:30-35
Leviticus 18:6-13
Deuteronomy 27:22
2 Samuel 13:1-22

lust

Genesis 19:1-29
Genesis 39:1-21
Judges 16:4-20
2 Samuel 11:2-5
Proverbs 6:20-35

Proverbs 7:1-27
Proverbs 23:26-28
Isaiah 57:5
Jeremiah 3:1-20
Ezekiel 23:1-49
Hosea 2:2-15
Nahum 3:4
Matthew 5:27-30
Romans 1:24-27
1 Corinthians 7:9
Ephesians 5:3
Colossians 3:5
1 Thessalonians 4:3-5
James 1:13-15

marital sex

Genesis 2:24
Genesis 4:1
Genesis 4:17
Genesis 29:21-30
Deuteronomy 22:13-21
Deuteronomy 24:5
Ruth 4:13
1 Samuel 1:19-20
2 Samuel 11:11
2 Samuel 12:24
1 Chronicles 2:21
1 Chronicles 7:23
Proverbs 5:15-20
Song of Songs (all)
Isaiah 8:3
Matthew 19:5
1 Corinthians 7:2-5

messy multi-marital sexual arrangements
Genesis 16:1-16
Genesis 29:21-30
Genesis 30:1-24
Genesis 38:1-30
2 Samuel 12:11

prostitution
Genesis 38:1-30
Leviticus 19:29
Judges 16:1
Proverbs 2:11-19
Proverbs 5:1-14
Proverbs 6:20-35
Proverbs 7:1-27
Proverbs 23:26-28
Jeremiah 3:1-20
Ezekiel 16:1-42
Ezekiel 23:1-49
Hosea 3:1-3
Hosea 4:10-19
Hosea 8:9
Hosea 9:1
Nahum 3:4
1 Corinthians 6:9-10
1 Corinthians 6:12-20

rape
Deuteronomy 22:25-29
Judges 19:16-30
2 Samuel 13:1-22

seduction
Genesis 19:30-35
Genesis 38:1-30

Genesis 39:1-21
Exodus 22:16
2 Samuel 11:2-5
Proverbs 2:11-19
Proverbs 5:1-20
Proverbs 6:20-35
Proverbs 7:1-27
Proverbs 23:26-28
Jeremiah 3:1-20
Ezekiel 16:1-42
Ezekiel 23:1-49
Nahum 3:4
James 1:13-15

sex with animals
Exodus 22:19
Leviticus 18:23
Leviticus 20:15-16

sleeping around
Genesis 35:22
Exodus 22:16
Leviticus 18:6-18, 20-22
Leviticus 19:20
Leviticus 20:10-13, 19-20
Numbers 5:11-31
Numbers 25:1-3
Deuteronomy 22:22-24
Deuteronomy 27:20, 23
1 Samuel 2:22
2 Samuel 11:2-5
2 Samuel 12:11
2 Samuel 16:20-22
Proverbs 5:1-20
Proverbs 6:20-35

Proverbs 7:1-27
Proverbs 23:26-28
Jeremiah 3:1-20
Ezekiel 16:1-42
Ezekiel 23:1-49
Hosea 1:2
Hosea 2:2-15
Matthew 15:19
Matthew 19:9
Mark 7:21
John 4:16
John 8:3-11
Acts 15:20, 29
Acts 21:25
Romans 1:24-27
Romans 13:13-14
1 Corinthians 5:1-2
1 Corinthians 6:9-10
1 Corinthians 6:12-20
1 Corinthians 10:8
2 Corinthians 12:21
Galatians 5:19-21
Ephesians 5:3
Colossians 3:5
1 Thessalonians 4:3-5
Jude 1:7
Revelation 2:14
Revelation 9:21
Revelation 21:8
Revelation 22:15

wet dreams
Leviticus 15:16-17
Leviticus 22:4
Deuteronomy 23:10-11

Notes

1. C. S. Lewis, *Mere Christianity* (New York: Collier Books/Macmillan, 1964), p. 96.
2. Mike Vance and Diane Deacon, *Think Out of the Box* (Franklin Lakes, NJ: Career Press, 1997), p. 138.
3. William Barclay, *The Gospel of Mark: The New Daily Study Bible.* (Louisville, KY: Westminster John Knox Press, 1975), p. 276.
4. Adapted from Eileen L. Zurbriggen, Rebecca L. Collins, Sharon Lamb, Tomi-Ann Roberts, Deborah L.Tolman, L. Monique Ward, and Jeanne Blake. Report of the APA Task Force on the Sexualization of Girls: Executive Summary (Washington, DC: APA, 2007), p. 2. http://www.apa.org/pi/wpo/sexualization.html (accessed July 14, 2008; see original document for the scholarship it refers to).
5. Kara Powell and Jim Hancock, *Good Sex: A Whole-Person Guide to Teenage Sexuality and God* (Grand Rapids, MI: Youth Specialties/Zondervan, 2009), pp. 77-78.
6. C. S. Lewis, *Letters of C. S. Lewis*, Harvest ed. (San Diego: Harcourt, 2003), p. 418.
7. Adapted from Dr. Laura Schlessinger, *Ten Stupid Things Women Do to Mess Up Their Lives*, 1st HarperPerennial ed., (New York: HarperCollins, 1995).
8. Adapted from Dr. Laura Schlessinger, *Ten Stupid Things Men Do to Mess Up Their Lives*, 1st HarperPerennial ed., (New York: HarperCollins, 1998).
9. Ernest Hemingway, *A Farewell to Arms* (New York: Scribner's and Sons, 1957), p. 249.
10. Mark Laaser, *Faithful and True: Sexual Integrity in a Fallen World* (Grand Rapids, MI: Zondervan, 1996), pp. 25-29.
11. Gerald May, *Addiction and Grace: Love and Spirituality in the Healing of Addictions* (New York: HarperCollins, 1998), p. 37.
12. Michael Kirk and Peter J. Boyer, "American Porn," *FRONTLINE* (aired February 7, 2002), http://www.pbs.org/wgbh/pages/frontline/shows/porn/ (accessed July 15, 2008).
13. Ibid.
14. Whitney Joiner, "Live Girl-on-Girl Action!" Salon.com, June 20, 2006, http://www.salon.com/mwt/feature/2006/06/20/girl_on_girl/print.html (accessed July 15, 2008).
15. Princeton Survey Research Associates International, "NBC News/People Magazine: National Survey of Young Teens Sexual Attitudes and Behaviors," January 26, 2005, http://www.msnbc.msn.com/id/6839080/ (accessed July 15, 2008).
16. Edward B. Pusey trans., *The Confessions of St. Augustine*, Book VIII, Chapter VII, Christian Classics Ethereal Library, http://www.ccel.org/ccel/augustine/confess.titlepage.html?highlight=confessions,augustine#highlight (accessed July 14, 2008).
17. William Barclay, *The Letter to the Romans*, rev. ed, (Louisville, KY: Westminster John Knox Press, 1975), pp.177-178.
18. The National Survey of Youth and Religion was reported in Christian Smith and Melinda Lundquist Denton, *Soul Searching: The Religious and Spiritual Lives of American Teenagers* (New York: Oxford University Press, 2005), Table 36 on p. 224.
19. Ibid.
20. Corrie ten Boom and Elizabeth and John Sherrill, *The Hiding Place*, 35th anniv. ed. (Grand Rapids, MI: Chosen Books, 2006), p. 227.
21. Ernest Hemingway, "The Capital of the World," in *The Complete Short Stories of Ernest Hemingway*, The Finca Vigía ed. (New York: Simon & Schuster, 1987), p. 29.
22. C. G. Jung, *Modern Man in Search of a Soul* (New York: Harcourt, Brace, 1933), p. 235.
23. Philip Elmer-Dewitt, "Now for the Truth About Americans and Sex," *Time*. (October 17, 1994), http://www.time.com/time/magazine/article/0,9171,981624,00.html (accessed July 16, 2008).
24. Centers for Disease Control and Prevention (CDC). *Tracking the Hidden Epidemics: Trends in STDs in the United States*, 2000. (Atlanta: U.S. Department of Health and Human Services, 2000).
25. L. Koutsky, "Epidemiology of Genital Human Papillomavirus Infection," *American Journal of Medicine* 102(5A), (1997): 3–8.

26. Henry J. Kaiser Family Foundation, "It's Your (Sex) Life: Your Guide to Safe and Responsible Sex," MTV Networks (2005): 18, http://www.mtv.com/thinkmtv/documents/IYSL.pdf (accessed July 16, 2008).

27. Lawrence Corey and H. Hunter Handsfield, "Genital Herpes and Public Health: Addressing a Global Problem," *Journal of the American Medical Association* 283, (2000): 791–794.

28. Roberta B. Ness et al., "Condom Use and the Risk of Recurrent Pelvic Inflammatory Disease, Chronic Pelvic Pain, or Infertility Following an Episode of Pelvic Inflammatory Disease," *American Journal of Public Health* 94, no. 8, (Aug. 2004): 1327–1329.

29. Janet S. St. Lawrence et al., "STD Screening, Testing, Case Reporting, and Clinical and Partner Notification Practices: A National Survey of U.S. Physicians," *American Journal of Public Health* 92, no. 11 (2002): 1784–1788.

30. Centers for Disease Control and Prevention (CDC). *HIV/AIDS Surveillance Report*, 2004. Vol. 16. (Atlanta: U.S. Department of Health and Human Services, 2005).

31. Henry J. Kaiser Family Foundation, "It's Your (Sex) Life: Your Guide to Safe and Responsible Sex," MTV Networks (2005): 18, http://www.mtv.com/thinkmtv/documents/IYSL.pdf (accessed July 16, 2008).

32. M. Glynn et al., "Estimated HIV Prevalence in the United States at the End of 2003," National HIV Prevention Conference in Atlanta (June 12-15, 2005).

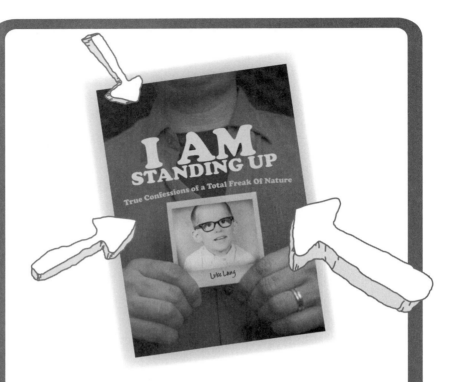

You'll laugh out loud at the embarrassing stories of Luke Lang, a self-proclaimed "freak of nature." While you're reading Luke's embarrassing stories—like the time he was beaten up by a girl in Karate class, or the time he was fighting for his life at Boy Scout camp—you'll learn a little about God's love and grace, and you'll be reminded that you were created on purpose, for a purpose.

I AM Standing Up
True Confessions of a Total Freak of Nature
Luke Lang
RETAIL $9.99
ISBN 978-0-310-28325-6

Everyone has secrets, but you don't have to live with your pain all alone. *Secret Survivors* tells the compelling, true stories of people who've lived through painful secrets. As you read stories about rape, addiction, cutting, abuse, abortion, and more, you'll find the strength to share your own story and start healing, and you may even discover how to help a friend in pain.

Secret Survivors
Real-Life Stories to Give You Hope for Healing
Jen Howver & Megan Hutchinson
RETAIL $12.99
ISBN 978-0-310-28322-5